SIMPLY NATURAL

Baby Food

Easy Recipes for Delicious Meals Your Infant and Toddler Will Love

Cathe Olson

goco Publishing
Nipomo, California

GOCO Publishing
Post Office Box 806
Nipomo, CA 93444
http://sweetandfizzy.com/catheskitchen/

The information in this booklet is meant to complement the advice and guidance of your pediatrician, not to replace it. Any application of the recommendations set forth in the following pages is at the reader's discretion and sole risk.

Cover design: sweetandfizzy.com

LCCN: 2002094166
ISBN: 0-9724690-3-6

Printed in the United States of America

Contents

Acknowledgments

Many people helped me in my quest to write this book. My parents, husband's parents, sisters, brother, brothers-in-law, and friends supported and encouraged me throughout the project.

Special thanks go to Dr. Hillel Janai, pediatrician, Dr. Susan Swadener, nutritionist, and Dr. Simon Cohen, naturopath, for reviewing the manuscript to ensure my information was accurate. Their advice was invaluable.

Thank you Hannah Rahill, publisher, for taking the time to read my work and offer advice. I am grateful to Jean Williams, Nina Rippy, and Gary Olson for their editing and proofreading help.

Thanks so much to Alexis Humphries who copy edited this book.

A huge thank you to Lissie Fein and Peter King for their tireless and amazing work designing the cover, creating the Cathe's Kitchen website, and helping in so many other ways.

Most of all, thanks to my wonderful family—Gary, Aimie and Emily—for their inspiration and constant appreciation for everything I cook.

Preface

After the birth of our first daughter, I decided to stay at home to rear our children and develop our organic vegetable/herb garden and fruit orchard.

Cooking continued to be a creative outlet for me. As I had primarily been cooking adult food for many years, preparing baby food was a new undertaking. The cookbooks available at my local natural foods store contained recipes calling for white flour, refined sugar, and processed foods. Most dishes required dairy products, eggs, or meat. No alternatives were provided for the vegetarian child. As I researched infant nutritional needs, I learned how important it is to give babies healthful food from the start and to establish good eating habits early.

I combined my knowledge of natural, whole foods cooking with what I had learned about infant nutrition to develop the recipes in this book. Since I understand that our lives are busy, I keep actual preparation time to a minimum. The cooking time for some meals is lengthy (i.e. grains and legumes) but since you don't have to be in the kitchen monitoring the meal, you are free to do other things. These recipes are all dishes that I prepare regularly. With two small children to care for, a garden and orchard to maintain, animals to tend, and books and articles to write, I don't want to spend my free time in the kitchen.

My daughters are enthusiastic, healthy eaters and have rarely been sick. I hope you find this book helpful with your children.

Introduction

Whole, unprocessed foods that you make yourself are healthiest for your child. Infants grow more rapidly than they will at any other period in their lives. At a time when nutrition is so important, most babies are being fed food from boxes and jars. Over-processed foods containing chemicals, preservatives, pesticide residue, and genetically engineered ingredients cannot nourish a growing child.

Make It Simple

You *can* make your own baby food. Even if you don't know how to cook, you will have no trouble following these easy recipes. The only equipment needed to puree infant meals is a blender or food processor.

This book contains practical recipes that can be incorporated into your busy day. Tips on cutting preparation time, helping baby to gain feeding independence, and getting maximum nutrition into baby's meals are interspersed throughout the book. Baby doesn't need complicated, gourmet meals. Your child will grow up appreciating the colors and flavors of fresh produce, whole grains and legumes, rather than craving the sugar and salt found in processed foods.

Make It Healthy

Relying on prepared baby food can be expensive, and your child may be exposed to unhealthy additives such as preservatives, pesticides and sodium. It is almost impossible to cook from scratch all of the time. Prepared foods or mixes are convenient when you don't have the time or energy to cook, but check labels carefully. Look for organic, all-natural foods with no additives. Avoid any product containing monosodium glutamate (MSG), hydrolyzed vegetable protein (HVP), autolyzed yeast, hydrogenated oils, high fructose corn syrup, caffeine, sulfites, artificial colors, artificial sweeteners, or preservatives. Although opinions differ, there are questions about the safety of these ingredients—especially for children. If you don't know what an ingredient is, you probably don't want it in your baby's food.

Make It Organic

Feed children organically grown food whenever possible. Infants are especially vulnerable to the effects of pesticides. Children experience rapid growth in a short period of time, and their brain and immune systems are immature. Safe dosage levels of pesticides are calculated based on adult tolerance, not children's. Crops are often treated with more than one chemical. The effects of these combinations are also untested. Pesticides are designed to kill insects or make them sterile so they can't reproduce. What effect might they have on your growing child? Contact the Environmental Working Group (see Sources and Resources) for more information. They publish a *Shopper's Guide to Pesticides in Produce*. It names the 12 most contaminated fruits and vegetables. Apples, grapes, and strawberries are on that list.

Commercially grown soybeans, most grains, and some fruits and vegetables are now genetically modified, and the list continues to grow. At the time of this writing, products containing genetically modified ingredients (GMOs) are not required to divulge that information on their labels. You must buy organic to ensure your food is GMO-free. Organic food is available at natural food stores, farmers' markets, and some supermarkets. If your market does not carry organic food, ask your grocer to stock or special order it for you.

Make It Fun

Enjoy your baby. This is the most miraculous, wonderful, amazing time you will ever know. Don't let mealtimes stress you out. If you want to spend extra time playing with your little one instead of cooking, don't feel guilty. You can always thaw one of the meals you froze, or use an emergency jar of food. Your infant needs love, attention, and a happy environment.

Involve older babies in the preparation of meals. There are ideas in the *Toddler Foods* section of this book for how a young child can help in the kitchen. In years to come, you will cherish the memories of this special time with your child.

How To Use This Book

This book provides general guidelines for starting your baby on solid foods, adding texture and finger foods, and graduating to table foods. It is helpful to get advice from books and your pediatrician, but the mother or primary caregiver is best equipped to decide when baby is ready for what foods. Don't worry if your baby is not where the books say she should be. Every baby develops at her own pace. Some babies take to eating more quickly, others take longer. Be observant and your baby will let you know what she needs.

Although the recipes in each section are designed for a specific age, older babies will continue to enjoy recipes from earlier sections. Babies that are chewing well may be ready for recipes in the *Older Baby Foods* or *Toddler Foods* sections.

For children on special diets, dishes without meat or dairy are offered, plus there are vegan alternatives for almost every recipe. For the child with wheat allergies, most of the baked goods in this book can be made with other grains.

Cooking for your baby can be enjoyable, as well as rewarding. Every chapter contains helpful tips designed to make your life easier. Don't be afraid to experiment by changing the recipes to suit your child's tastes. Creating new recipes can be as much fun as eating them.

Equipment

A food processor or blender is necessary to prepare many of the recipes in this book. A baby food grinder and seed grinder are also nice to have, but your processor or blender can perform the same tasks.

Food Processor: Food processors are versatile for making baby food. You can puree foods to different textures and make big batches at one time. They work better than blenders when your child is ready for more substance in his food. In addition, they mince, chop, shred, and slice foods. This saves time when preparing soups, casseroles, salads, etc. They are excellent for grinding nuts and seeds to different textures and for making nut and seed butters. You can even mix up bread, cake, muffin, or cookie dough in them.

Blender: A blender is the best choice for making smoothies. It is also great for grinding nuts, seeds and grains to a fine powder. Use a blender to puree baby's first solid foods because it produces the smoothest texture.

Baby Food Grinder: Small, hand grinders are inexpensive and convenient at home, at restaurants, and while traveling. They quickly and easily mash small amounts of table food to produce meal-size portions. *Hand grinders do not produce a smooth enough texture for baby's first purees.*

Seed Grinder: Seed or coffee grinders can quickly grind small amounts of nuts, seeds, and grains to a fine powder for cereals and baking.

Ingredients

Beans and Legumes: Buy organic, unprocessed beans (lentils, split peas, black beans, etc.). They are a good source of protein, B vitamins, and minerals such as calcium and iron. Beans are inexpensive, keep well, and are very filling. Beans and legumes can be introduced when baby is 7 to 9 months old.

Breads: Give your baby whole grain bread. In addition to having no nutritional value, white bread can cause choking. Read the label carefully when buying bread. Even whole grain breads may contain artificial colors, additives, and preservatives. *Ezekiel Breads* are an excellent choice. They are made with organic, sprouted grains and contain no preservatives. Bread can be introduced when baby is 7 months old.

Crackers: Buy soft crackers made with whole grain flour that do not contain hydrogenated oils, sugar, or sodium such as *Barbara's Wheatines*. This book contains several easy cracker recipes so you can make your own. Crackers can be introduced when baby is 7 months old.

Cultured and Fermented Foods: Fermented foods contain enzymes and healthy bacteria that aid digestion. Miso, amasake, yogurt, kefir, and cottage cheese are foods that young children can easily digest. High temperatures kill the live enzymes, so never boil these foods. Cultured and fermented foods can be introduced when baby is 10 to 12 months old.

Dairy Products and Substitutes: When introducing your infant to dairy products, start with yogurt or cottage cheese. They contain enzymes that make them easier for baby to digest. Milk is not usually given until a child is one year old. Buy organic dairy products to ensure that the cows were not given hormones, antibiotics, or pesticide-treated feed. Do not give baby low-fat or nonfat dairy products. Serve soft, unripened cheeses such as cottage, cream, farmer, ricotta, and mozzarella. Hard, aged cheeses (such as cheddar or swiss) are hard to digest and contain large amounts of sodium. Serve only small amounts of hard cheeses to infants. Avoid processed and imitation cheeses. They contain additives and preservatives. Soy, rice, and almond substitutes can be used to replace dairy in any of the recipes in this book. Dairy products can be introduced when baby is 9 to 12 months old.

Eggs: Eggs contain protein, iron, and most vitamins and minerals. They can be allergenic, so pediatricians recommend waiting until baby is 10 to 12 months old. Since egg whites seem to cause most problems, serve yolks alone before proceeding to whole eggs. Buy organic, free range eggs. They are free of chemical residue and contain more vitamin A. *Ener-G Egg Replacer* (available at natural food stores) may be used instead of eggs in baking. Eggs can be introduced when baby is 10 to 12 months old.

Fish: Fish is easy to digest and is an excellent source of protein, vitamins, and minerals. Salmon and other cold-water fish are especially beneficial because they contain omega-3 essential fatty acids which are important for brain development. Always remove bones and chop well. Fish can be introduced when baby is 10 months old.

Fruit: Fresh fruit is best. If unavailable, use frozen. Canned should be the last choice because of the added sodium and sugar, as well as the overprocessing caused by the canning procedure itself. *Buy organic.* Most produce is heavily sprayed and washing doesn't remove all the residue. Peel non-organic fruit before eating, especially those with a waxy finish. Generally, domestic produce contains fewer chemicals than imported. Buy local when you can't get organic. Fruit can be introduced when baby is 4 to 7 months old.

Grains: Use organic whole grains (brown rice, millet, quinoa, barley, etc.). Whole grains are good sources of protein, B vitamins and minerals. They are nutritious, inexpensive, and keep well. Grain cereals can be introduced when baby is 4 to 7 months old. Whole grains can be introduced when baby is 7 to 10 months old.

Herbs: Many recipes call for dried herbs—but if you have fresh, by all means, use them. Substitute dried herbs with three times as much fresh (i.e. 1 teaspoon dried = 1 tablespoon fresh). *Parsley* is an especially nutritious herb. It contains lots of vitamins A and C and is a good source of iron. The vitamin C helps the iron to be absorbed. Parsley can be introduced when baby is 7 months old. Introduce other herbs after baby is 9 months old.

Nuts and Seeds: Nuts and seeds are excellent sources of protein, vitamins, minerals, and essential fatty acids. Infants should never be given whole nuts because of the danger of choking. Peanuts and other round nuts pose an especially high risk. Chopped nuts and seeds are great in baked goods and cereals. Flax seeds and walnuts contain omega-3 essential fatty acids. Grind nuts and seeds in your blender, food processor or seed grinder.

Nut and seed butters are wonderful on toast, crackers, or as a dip for veggies. Almond butter and tahini (sesame butter) are high in calcium. When buying nut and seed butters, avoid products with additives such as hydrogenated oils or sugar. Many natural food stores offer machines that grind whole nuts to butter while you wait, guaranteeing you a fresh product with no additives. Nuts and seeds can be introduced when baby is 10 months old.

Oil and Butter: Olive and flax oils contain omega-3 essential fatty acids which are important for baby's brain development. Use these oils instead of butter on cooked grains, toast, vegetables, etc. to add flavor and nutrition. Cold-pressed or expeller-pressed canola and safflower oils are good choices for baking and stir-fries. Use real butter rather than margarine which usually contains hydrogenated oils and chemicals. Avoid palm oil, coconut oil, cocoa butter, and hydrogenated oils. Oil and butter can be introduced when baby is 10 months old.

Poultry: Organic poultry can be given in moderation to older infants. It provides protein, vitamins, zinc, and iron. Always remove bones and chop well. Poultry may be introduced when baby is 10 months old.

Nutritional Yeast: This non-leavening yeast is a complete protein and a good source of B vitamins. Look for yeast fortified with vitamin B-12 if your family follows a vegan diet. Nutritional yeast has a savory, cheesy taste. It comes in flakes and is usually available in bulk at natural food stores. Nutritional yeast can be introduced when baby is 10 months old.

Sea Vegetables: Sea vegetables are exceptional sources of minerals, vitamins, and protein. They help strengthen bones and teeth, and improve nerve transmission and digestion. Sea Veg Mix (page 56) makes it easy to incorporate sea vegetables into your baby's meals. Dried sea vegetables are available at natural food stores.

Agar Agar is a natural gelatin that is rich in calcium, iron, and other minerals and vitamins.

Arame, Hiziki (also *Hijiki*), *Kelp*, and *Wakame* are excellent sources of calcium as well as other vitamins and minerals.

Kombu tenderizes food, enhances flavors, and is rich in vitamins and minerals. Add a strip when cooking beans to soften them and make them easier to digest.

Sea Vegetables can be introduced when baby is 10 months old.

Sodium: Bragg Liquid Aminos, low-sodium tamari or shoyu soy sauce, miso, and kelp (a sea vegetable) are healthy sodium alternatives available at natural food stores.

Bragg Liquid Aminos are similar to soy sauce but are not fermented and contain no additives.

Choose low-sodium *tamari* or *shoyu* soy sauces because they are naturally fermented. Avoid common soy sauce. It is chemically fermented and contains additives and coloring, and may even contain additional salt. Some soy sauces contain wheat so check the label if your child is allergic to it.

Miso is a naturally fermented soy product. It is a good source of protein because it contains eight amino acids. Its salty, sweet taste adds flavor to soups, sauces, and salad dressings. Buy only unpasteurized, naturally fermented miso. Miso is made from a variety of grains or beans and ranges from white to deep brown. Basically, the lighter the color, the sweeter and lighter the taste.

Granulated or powdered *kelp* is very high in minerals, including calcium and iodine.

Regular table salt contains additives. Try *sea salt* instead.

Use sodium products sparingly as baby's kidneys cannot handle much sodium. Sodium products can be introduced when baby is 10 months old.

Sweeteners: Fruit, juice, juice concentrate, honey, brown rice syrup, pure maple syrup, and molasses are suggested to sweeten food. No matter which sweetener you choose, use it sparingly. They are all, in effect, sugar. Honey should not be given to infants until 12 months of age. Never give artificial sweeteners to a child and avoid them if you are pregnant or nursing. Saccharin has been shown to cause cancer in animals and many reports of adverse reactions to aspartame have been filed with the FDA. Do not give any sweetener other than fruit or juice before baby is 10 months old.

Vegetables: Fresh vegetables are best. If unavailable, use frozen. Canned should be the last choice because of the added sodium and the overprocessing caused by the canning procedure itself. *Buy organic.* Most produce is heavily sprayed and washing doesn't remove all the residue. Peel non-organic vegetables before eating, especially those with a waxy finish. Generally, domestic produce contains fewer chemicals than imported. If you can't get organic, buy local. Vegetables can be introduced when baby is 4 to 7 months old.

Soy Products: Soy products are a good protein choice for vegetarians. Some products may be found in supermarkets, but the greatest selection is available at natural food stores.

Tofu is especially digestible, making it ideal for infants. It is a good source of calcium and iron and is low in sodium. Use firm tofu in recipes unless otherwise specified. Soft or silken tofu works well in puddings or purees.

Tempeh has a meaty, chewy texture that makes it a good substitute for beef or chicken. It is a fermented product that contains vitamin B-12.

Textured Vegetable Protein (TVP) comes in dried flakes. It becomes soft and chewy—similar to diced chicken or ground beef—when mixed with boiling water or broth.

Soy products can be introduced when baby is 10 months old.

☺Tip: Buy whole foods in bulk. Not only will it save you money, but by minimizing the amount of packaging, you will help preserve the environment for our children.☺

Vegetarian Babies

There are many benefits to a vegetarian diet. Commercial meat and poultry may contain pesticide, antibiotic, and chemical residue. Meat is high in saturated fat and cholesterol and is hard to digest. Vegetarian children have no problem getting the fat and protein they need from plants, dairy products, and eggs. Vegans, who avoid all animal products, must be conscious of food choices for their children. Adequate protein, calcium, iron, fat, and calories are necessary for your baby to thrive.

Children need food for energy, health, and to support their growth and development. Do not feed your baby junk food. Every mouthful your child takes should be nutritious. Parents must be diligent about providing a variety of beans, grains, vegetables, fruits, nuts, seeds, and oils. Vitamin B-12 is difficult to obtain from plants. Be sure to serve fortified nutritional yeast flakes, tempeh, miso, and sea vegetables on a regular basis. Your infant's diet must include adequate fat. Avocados, nuts, seeds, and whole-fat soy products are good choices. Olive, flax, and canola oils contain omega-3 essential fatty acids, which are important for proper brain development. Read *New Vegetarian Baby* (see Sources and Resources) for more information.

Most of the recipes in this book are vegetarian. The recipes that contain fish or poultry specify vegetarian alternatives. There are lots of creative dishes made with grains, beans, nuts, seeds, and sea vegetables to nourish the vegetarian and vegan baby.

Starting

Solids

Four to Seven Months

Babies usually start eating solid foods by the time they are seven months old. Do not feed baby solids earlier than four months of age as that increases the risk of allergic reactions. Infants instinctively know when they are ready to start eating solid foods. Baby will watch your food as it travels from plate to mouth. She may even try to grab a morsel. Since baby's diet will consist of breast milk or formula for many more months, these first tastes are just to get her accustomed to new foods. *Never force your baby to eat.* Offer a small amount of food on a baby or demitasse spoon. Hold it between baby's lips, and let her suck the food off. Stop when she turns away or closes her mouth. One or two tablespoons of food is plenty. At this age, food should not replace her regular feedings. It is best not to try solids when baby is ravenous. Try after a feeding or at a family meal. Never feed baby pureed food in a bottle. The unfamiliar texture may cause choking.

Each new food you introduce to baby should be offered alone (or with a food already introduced successfully), so if there's a sensitivity or allergy, you will recognize it. Wait three to five days before introducing the next food. Allergic reactions may include bloating, gassiness, diarrhea, rash around mouth or anus, or runny nose not associated with a cold. Do not introduce a new food if baby is sick. You will not know if reactions are from illness or food.

This section contains recipes for baby's first cereals and purees.

First Solid Foods

Babies are often started on rice cereal mixed with water, breast milk, or formula. The cereal has a mild taste and is unlikely to cause allergic reactions. Here are some other good first food choices.

barley cereal	green beans	apples	avocados
millet cereal	squash	peaches	bananas
oat cereal	sweet potatoes	pears	
rice cereal	zucchini		

Note: Acidic foods such as citrus, berries, and tomatoes should be avoided because they can be allergenic to some babies. Salt, sugar, and spices should not be added to food.

☺Tip: Avocado is an excellent first food choice. It is quick to prepare, easy for baby to eat, and contains fats that baby needs. Unlike rice cereal and bananas, it does not cause constipation.☺

Preparation

Cereals: Make your own cereal (recipes follow), or buy cereal specifically made for babies. Mix prepared cereal with room temperature water, breast milk, or formula. Do not add fruit or sweeteners or your baby may begin to reject unsweetened foods.
Vegetables: Steam vegetables over boiling water, or simmer in a little water until soft and mushy. You must overcook vegetables in order for them to puree well. Pour vegetables and some of the cooking water in blender. Puree until smooth. Add more water to achieve desired consistency. Do not add any fat or seasonings. Make extra to freeze.

Fruit: Simmer fruit in a little water until soft. Pour fruit and some of the cooking water in blender. Puree until smooth. Add more water to achieve desired consistency. Do not add sweeteners.

Avocado and Bananas: Peel very ripe avocado or banana, and mash with a fork until smooth. Thin with a little water, breast milk, or formula if desired.

☺Tip: Pumping extra milk to mix into baby's food is inconvenient and time-consuming. It is much easier to use water. As long as baby is still nursing or drinking formula, she does not need the extra milk.☺

Storage

Baby food can be refrigerated for several days or frozen for several months. To save time when making your own baby food, prepare large batches. Keep enough in the refrigerator for the next day or two, and freeze the rest. Use small plastic containers or recycled baby food jars to freeze meal-size portions. Another easy storage method is to pour food into ice cube trays. When frozen, pop cubes out and store in freezer bag or plastic container. They are perfect when you need a meal in a hurry because they thaw quickly, and you can take out only as much as you need.

Warm refrigerated or frozen food in hot-water bath. Place heat-proof jar or bowl in a pan. Fill pan with water to one inch below top of container. Warm over medium heat until food is room temperature.

IMPORTANT NOTE

Place a small amount of food in baby's bowl. You can always add more. Once food has come in contact with baby's mouth, spoon, or fingers, it cannot be saved for a later feeding. Any leftover food that has been touched must be discarded.

Homemade Baby Cereals

Many parents choose packaged baby cereals because they are iron-fortified. Typically, babies will not deplete the supply of iron they were born with until six months of age. If baby is breastfeeding, it may be even later because the iron in breast milk is so well assimilated. Foods containing iron will be introduced when baby is comfortable eating solid foods.

Homemade cereal is less processed and fresher than packaged cereal. To save time, prepare enough for several feedings. For emergencies, you may want to keep a box of packaged baby cereal on hand. It is easy to take along and can be mixed with banana, avocado, or applesauce for a quick meal.

Ground Rice, Barley, Quinoa, or Millet Cereal

In dry skillet over medium heat, toast **1 to 2 cups brown rice, barley, quinoa, or millet** for 10 minutes, stirring occasionally. Grains should begin to pop. Cool completely. Store in covered jar.

To serve: Grind desired amount of toasted grain to fine powder in seed grinder or blender. Whisk together **1 part cereal powder** and **6 parts water**. Bring to a boil, and simmer uncovered for 30 to 40 minutes, or until soft and smooth.

Variation: For the rest of the family, use **1 part cereal** to **4 parts water**. Cook 15 to 20 minutes.

Cooked Rice Cereal

Place ½ **cup brown rice** in **3 cups water**. Cover and bring to a boil over high heat. Reduce heat and simmer for one hour. Rice should be very soft, so cook longer if necessary. It is okay if water is not completely absorbed. Puree cereal in blender. Add extra water if needed for a thin, smooth texture. Refrigerate or freeze extra cereal.

☺Tip: To heat up refrigerated leftovers, mix desired amount of food with boiling water. The water will thin it out and bring the food to room temperature.☺

Baby Oatmeal

Place **1 to 2 cups rolled oats** in blender or food processor. Grind to fine powder. Store in covered jar.

To serve: Whisk together **1 part oat powder** and **3 parts water**. Bring to a boil and simmer uncovered for 15 minutes, or until soft and smooth. Add more water if necessary for a thin texture.

Intermediate

Foods

Seven to Ten Months

By seven months, baby is becoming more interested in food. Instead of little tastes, he wants actual meals. At seven months, feed baby solid foods twice a day. By nine months, your child can eat solids three times a day. Include baby at family meals as much as possible. Let baby hold a spoon even if he just plays with it. Encourage your infant to eat with his fingers. Place some finger food on his tray. He may make a mess, but the sooner your baby is able to feed himself, the easier it will be for you.

Add texture to baby's food. Use a food processor or baby food grinder to puree meals. Soft foods can be mashed with a fork. It is still a good idea not to add salt or sweeteners.

Iron is becoming important as baby depletes the supply of iron he was born with. Iron-rich foods to add to baby's diet include: parsley, green leafy vegetables, sweet potatoes, apricots, and easily digestible legumes such as adzuki beans, lentils, and peas.

Infant's tastes change from day to day and from meal to meal. Baby may devour carrots at lunch and spit them out at supper. Don't base food likes or dislikes on one experience. Put a small amount of food in baby's bowl. You can always add more if he wants it, but it's a shame to throw away food you spent time preparing.

Give baby a sippy cup of water with each meal. At first, you will have to help, but it won't take long before he'll be able to drink by himself. You can wean baby directly from breast to cup.

☺Tip: It is never too early to start good dental hygiene. Wipe or brush baby's teeth after every meal even if it feels silly just to brush one or two teeth.☺

Fruits and Vegetables

Mashed Raw Fruit

Ripe fruit can be mashed and eaten raw. Try fruit alone or mixed with cereal.

½ cup diced raw pear, peach, mango, papaya, melon, or banana

Remove peel and seeds. Mash with a fork or baby food grinder.

Yield: 1 serving

Note: Fruit must be soft and ripe.

Pear-Applesauce

1 pear, peeled and diced
1 apple, peeled and diced
½ cup water

Place fruit and water in pan. Cover and simmer over low heat until soft. Add more water if necessary to keep fruit from scorching. Puree or mash.

Yield: About 2 cups

Sweet Potato and Green Beans

1 sweet potato, diced
¼ cup chopped green beans

Place vegetables in pan with 1 inch of water. Cover and simmer until soft. Puree or mash.

Yield: About 2 cups

Purple Puree

1 cup chopped red cabbage
1 carrot, sliced
½ apple, peeled, cored, and sliced
1 tablespoon raisins

Place cabbage, carrot, apple, and raisins in pan with 1 inch of water. Cover and simmer over low heat until soft. Puree in blender, food processor, or baby food grinder.

Yield: About 2 cups

Squash and Peas

2 cups peeled and cubed winter squash
½ cup peas

Place vegetables in pan with 1 inch of water. Cover and simmer over low heat until soft. Puree or mash.

Yield: About 2 cups

Potato and Greens

1 potato, diced
¼ cup minced greens or cabbage

Place potato and greens in pan with 1 inch of water. Cover and simmer over low heat until soft. Mash with fork or baby food grinder.

Yield: About 1 cup

Note: Never use green or sprouted potatoes. The poisonous alkaloids can be harmful to infants.

Cauliflower and Broccoli

½ cup chopped cauliflower
½ cup chopped broccoli

Place vegetables in pan with ½ inch of water. Cover and simmer until very soft. Puree or mash.

Yield: About 1 cup

Carrots and Beans

Baby will love the sweet taste of beans and carrots.

2 cups thickly sliced carrots (about 3 carrots)
¼ cup adzuki beans
¼ strip kombu sea vegetable
1½ cups water

Place all ingredients in pan. Cover and bring to a boil. Simmer 60 minutes, or until beans are tender. Puree or mash.

Yield: About 2½ cups

Root Vegetable Mash

1 rutabaga, peeled and diced
1 potato, peeled and diced
1 tablespoon fresh minced parsley

Place vegetables in pan with 1 inch of water. Cover and simmer over low heat until soft. Add parsley and mash with a fork or baby food grinder.

Yield: About 2 cups

Grains

When baby is comfortable with a little texture, whole grains may be added to his diet. Start with small grains like rolled oats, millet, quinoa, and short grain brown rice. Grain recipes for infants are prepared with extra water to make them soft and mushy. You may even want to grind them with your food processor or baby food grinder at first. As baby gets more experience with solid foods, you can gradually reduce the water so the grains will be firmer.

Rolled Oats

Rolled oats are high in protein and easy to digest. The slow-cooking variety is more nutritious than quick-cooking or instant oats because it is less processed.

Cooking Rolled Oats for Infants

Place **½ cup rolled oats** and **1½ cups water** in pan. Simmer uncovered over low heat for 20 minutes, or until desired thickness is achieved.

Yield: 1 cup

Applesauce Oatmeal

Cook rolled oats as above. Mix in **1 tablespoon unsweetened applesauce** per ¼ cup cooked rolled oats.

Yield: 1 serving

Banana Oatmeal

Cook rolled oats as above. Mix in **1 tablespoon mashed banana** per ¼ cup cooked rolled oats.

Yield: 1 serving

Tofu Oatmeal

Cook rolled oats as above. Mix in **1 tablespoon mashed tofu** per ¼ cup cooked rolled oats.

Yield: 1 serving

Instant Baby Cereal

Homemade cereal is economical and nutritious. I've added parsley for iron, calcium, and vitamin C. These nutrients are important now that baby is drinking less breast milk or formula.

Place **2 cups rolled oats** and **2 tablespoons dried parsley** in your food processor with metal blade. Grind to powder. Store in covered jar.

Yield: About 1¾ cups

To serve: Pour desired amount of cereal in bowl. Cover with boiling water. Stir in a little breast milk, formula, or water for a thinner texture.

Millet

Infants love the sweet, nutty taste of millet. The small grain is easy to chew, and millet is a good source of protein, vitamins, and minerals. It cooks quickly so it's convenient to make. Baby will love millet plain or in any of the variations below.

Cooking Millet for Infants

Pour **1 cup millet** and **4 cups water** in pan. Cover and bring to boil over high heat. Reduce heat to low. Simmer 30 minutes.

Yield: 3½ cups

Quick Millet and Applesauce

¼ cup cooked millet
1 tablespoon applesauce

Mix warm millet with applesauce.

Yield: 1 serving

Millet and Squash

1 cup peeled and cubed winter squash
½ cup millet
3½ cups water
2 tablespoons fresh minced parsley

Place squash, millet, and water in pan. Cover and bring to boil over high heat. Reduce heat to low and simmer 30 minutes. Add parsley. Puree or mash.

Yield: 2¼ cups

Millet and Peaches

½ cup millet
1 peach, diced
2 cups water

Place all ingredients in pan. Cover and bring to boil over high heat. Reduce heat to low. Simmer 25 to 30 minutes, or until water is absorbed. Puree or mash.

Yield: 2 cups

☺Tip: Make enough rice, millet, or quinoa to last two or three days. Leftover grains can make a meal in seconds. Pour a little boiling water over the cold grains and let sit a minute or two before serving to baby. Cooked grains may also be frozen.☺

Millet and Peas

½ cup millet
½ cup peas (fresh or frozen)
2 cups water

Place all ingredients in pan. Cover and bring to boil over high heat. Reduce heat to low and simmer 30 minutes. Puree or mash.

Yield: 2 cups

Quinoa

Quinoa contains the highest amount of protein of any grain. It is especially high in lysine, which is hard to obtain from plant foods. Quinoa contains many other vital nutrients, including calcium and iron. It is a small grain and easy to digest.

Cooking Quinoa for Infants

Pour **1 cup quinoa** and **4 cups water** in pan. Cover and bring to boil over high heat. Reduce heat to low. Simmer 30 minutes.

Yield: 3½ cups

Quick Quinoa and Avocado

¼ cup cooked quinoa
¼ avocado

Mash quinoa with avocado.

Yield: 1 serving

Quinoa and Grated Vegetables

¼ cup grated zucchini
¼ cup grated carrots
½ cup quinoa
2 cups water

Place all ingredients in pan. Cover and bring to boil over high heat. Reduce heat to low. Simmer 30 minutes.

Yield: 2 cups

Quinoa and Sweet Potatoes

1 sweet potato, peeled and diced
½ cup quinoa
3½ cups water
2 tablespoons fresh minced parsley

Place sweet potatoes, quinoa, and water in pan. Cover and bring to boil over high heat. Reduce heat to low and simmer 30 minutes. Add parsley. Puree or mash.

Yield: 2¼ cups

Quinoa and Cauliflower

½ cup quinoa
1 cup chopped cauliflower
2¼ cups water

Place quinoa, cauliflower, and water in pan. Cover and bring to boil over high heat. Reduce heat to low. Simmer 30 minutes.

Yield: About 2 cups

Brown Rice

Of all the grains, brown rice supplies the highest concentration of B vitamins. It is also a good source of iron, vitamin E, and protein. It comes in long-grain, short-grain, basmati, and sweet varieties. Short-grain brown rice is a good choice to start with. All types of rice can be prepared for baby as follows.

Cooking Brown Rice for Infants

Pour **1 cup brown rice** and **3 cups water** in pan. Cover and bring to boil over high heat. Reduce heat to low. Simmer 50 minutes.

Yield: 2½ cups

Rice and Lentils

This dish supplies lots of iron.

½ cup lentils
½ cup brown rice
1 carrot, diced
3 cups water

Place all ingredients in pan. Cover and bring to a boil over high heat. Reduce heat and simmer for 60 minutes. Add more water if needed to prevent scorching. Puree or mash.

Yield: 2½ cups

Rice and Greens

½ cup brown rice
½ cup chopped kale, collard greens, or chard
1½ cups water

Place all ingredients in pan. Cover and bring to boil over high heat. Reduce heat and simmer for 50 minutes. Puree or mash.

Yield: 1½ cups

Rice and Veggies

½ cup brown rice
½ cup chopped broccoli or cauliflower
2 cups water

Place all ingredients in pan. Cover and bring to boil over high heat. Reduce heat to low and simmer for 50 minutes. Puree or mash.

Yield: 1½ cups

Rice and Tofu

1 cup cooked brown rice
2 ounces tofu, diced
1 tablespoon fresh minced parsley

Mash or grind rice with tofu and parsley.

Yield: 1¼ cups

Finger Foods

Give your baby finger foods at every meal so he can learn to feed himself. (They will also keep him busy while you take a few bites of your own meal.) Choose foods that baby can gum to swallowable consistency or that will dissolve in his mouth without chewing. It is best to place only a few pieces on baby's plate or high chair tray at a time. This prevents baby from stuffing too much food into his mouth. Because of the danger of choking, baby should always be seated when eating and should never be left unattended.

First Finger Foods

- Whole grain bread chunks
- Diced avocado
- Diced banana
- Diced soft, very ripe fruit (mango, peach, cantaloupe, etc.)
- Diced, cooked (very soft) vegetables (squash, potatoes, carrots, broccoli, or cauliflower, etc.)
- Rice cakes
- Soft crackers
- Well-cooked pasta
- Cereal "O's" (organic, whole grain O's with less than 4 grams of sugar per serving like *Oatios*)

Foods to Avoid (Choking Risk)

- Uncooked raisins
- Whole grapes
- Popcorn
- Nuts
- Whole peas
- Raw firm-fleshed fruit or vegetables

Rice-Oat Crackers

These light, flaky crackers are perfect for infants because they contain no wheat, salt, or sweeteners. The only problem is keeping the rest of the family from eating them all!

**1½ cups rolled oats
1 cup brown rice flour (or whole wheat)
Pinch kelp
¼ cup canola or safflower oil
½ cup water**

Preheat oven to 350°. Oil baking sheet. Grind oats to a coarse powder in food processor or blender. Mix oats with flour and kelp. Stir in oil until mixture resembles coarse crumbs. Add water and knead lightly until combined.

Roll or press dough to ⅛-inch thickness on prepared baking sheet. Score into squares, and prick with fork. Bake 15 to 20 minutes, or until edges are slightly brown. The longer you bake, the crispier the crackers will be. Cool crackers before removing from pan. They will harden slightly as they cool.

Yield: About 3 dozen

Zwieback

This teething toast is simple to make.

Preheat oven to 250°. Cut **½-inch thick slices of bread** into strips about 1½ inches wide. Place on unoiled baking sheet. Bake one hour, or until strips are dried out and hard.

Older Baby

Foods

Ten to Fourteen Months

By ten months, your baby should be adept at finger feeding. Try not to worry about the mess. Use a big bib, and spread a plastic tarp or newspaper under the high chair. Offer a variety of foods, and let baby try food off your plate. Solid food is now reducing or replacing baby's regular feedings, so protein, fat, calcium, and iron are important. Sea vegetables, nuts, and seeds are included in many recipes to provide these nutrients.

Baby can begin to eat poultry and fish, as well as yogurt and cheese. Cow's milk is not normally given until baby is one year old because it is hard to digest. Eggs may be given between 10 and 12 months. Give baby well-cooked yolks first, since the whites can be allergenic. Continue to introduce new foods one at a time.

You may also begin using small amounts of herbs, spices, butter, and oil. By 12 to 14 months, baby should be eating most of the same foods as the rest of the family. Until your child is adept at spoon-feeding, serve lots of finger foods.

☺Tip: To encourage baby to spoon-feed herself, serve a bowl of her favorite food with a small, easy-to-manage spoon. Try applesauce, yogurt, mashed sweet squash, etc.☺

Breakfast Foods

Cornmeal Mush

½ cup cornmeal
Pinch kelp
2 cups water

Mix cornmeal, kelp, and water together in pan. Bring to a boil over medium heat, stirring constantly. Reduce heat to low. Continue stirring and simmer a few minutes to achieve desired consistency. Serve plain or with milk, flax oil, or yogurt.

Yield: 3 servings

Millet Porridge

1 cup millet
1 teaspoon Sea Veg Mix (page 56) or pinch kelp
1 teaspoon ground cinnamon
1 tablespoon ground almonds or sesame seeds
5 cups water

Place all ingredients in pan and bring to a boil. Reduce heat and simmer uncovered 30 minutes. Stir occasionally to prevent sticking.

Yield: 4 to 6 servings

Milk Toast

Place **2 to 3 pieces Zwieback** (page 40) or **1 slice whole grain toast cut into quarters** in a bowl. Cover Zwieback or toast with **hot milk** (dairy or non-dairy). Sprinkle with **ground cinnamon**.

Yield: 1 serving

Instant Older Baby Cereal

This cereal provides protein, fat, calcium, iron, and other important vitamins and minerals to supplement baby's diet as she weans off breast milk or formula.

**½ cup raw, hulled sunflower seeds or almonds
2 cups rolled oats
1½ tablespoons dried parsley**

Grind sunflower seeds or almonds to a powder in food processor or blender. Add rolled oats and dried parsley. Grind to a coarse powder. Store in covered jar.

Yield: 2 cups

To serve: Pour desired amount of cereal in a bowl. Cover with boiling water. Stir in milk, yogurt or cottage cheese if desired.

Fruity Cereal

Pour ¼ **cup Instant Older Baby Cereal** into bowl. Cover with boiling water. Stir ¼ **cup diced ripe peach, nectarine, or apricot** into cereal.

Yield: 1 serving

Avocado-Cereal Mash

Pour ¼ **cup Instant Older Baby Cereal** into bowl. Cover with boiling water. Mash ¼ **avocado** into cereal.

Yield: 1 serving

Cottage Cheese and Applesauce

¼ cup cottage cheese
1 tablespoon unsweetened applesauce
1 tablespoon wheat germ

Mix cottage cheese and applesauce together. Sprinkle with wheat germ.

Yield: 1 serving

Baby Egg Breakfast

This breakfast is easy for baby to eat with her fingers when eggs and toast are cut into small pieces.

1 whole egg (or 2 egg yolks)
Dash water
Pinch nutritional yeast flakes
Pinch kelp
1 slice whole grain toast
Olive oil, flax oil, or butter

Beat egg with water, nutritional yeast flakes, and kelp. Pour into small skillet with a little oil over medium heat. Stir gently until firm. Spread oil or butter on toast.

Yield: 1 serving

Apple-Oat Pancakes

Soy, rice, or almond milk can be used in this recipe if baby is not drinking cow's milk.

> **1¾ cups rolled oats**
> **¼ cup almonds**
> **1 teaspoon baking powder**
> **½ teaspoon ground cinnamon**
> **2 eggs (or 4 egg yolks)**
> **1⅓ cups milk (dairy or non-dairy)**
> **1 apple, grated**

Grind oats and nuts to powder in blender or food processor. Pour oat mixture into a large mixing bowl and stir in baking powder and cinnamon.

Beat eggs and milk together. Grate apple in food processor or by hand. Add the egg mixture and apple to oats. Stir until just mixed. Let batter sit 5 minutes while griddle heats.

Bake pancakes on a lightly oiled griddle or skillet over medium heat. Use approximately ¼ cup batter for each pancake. Cook for 5 minutes. Turn when top is bubbly and edges are starting to dry. Cook for 3 to 5 more minutes.

Yield: 12 pancakes

☺Tip: Leftover pancakes can be refrigerated or frozen. They can be eaten warm or cold for a quick snack or meal.☺

Banana Johnnycakes

These pancakes are just as quick to prepare as those from a store-bought mix.

 1 cup cornmeal
 Pinch sea salt
 1¼ cups boiling water
 2 teaspoons molasses or honey
 1 banana, peeled and sliced

Place cornmeal and salt in heat-proof mixing bowl. Whisk in boiling water and sweetener. Add bananas and stir gently. If batter is too thick, add a little water or milk.

Bake cakes on a lightly oiled griddle or skillet over medium heat. Use approximately ⅛ cup batter for each cake. Cook 5 minutes. Turn when edges begin to dry. Do not turn prematurely. Cook 3 to 5 more minutes. Remove from pan. Keep in warm oven until ready to serve.

Yield: 10 pancakes

Fruity Yogurt

 ¼ cup plain yogurt
 ¼ cup diced fruit (peaches, apricots, banana, etc.)
 2 tablespoons Instant Older Baby Cereal (page 44)

Mix yogurt and fruit together. Sprinkle with cereal.

Yield: 1 serving

Soups

Baby Chicken Soup (Regular or Vegetarian)

Minced vegetables make this soup easy for baby to eat.

½ onion, chopped
1 clove garlic, minced
2 medium carrots, diced
2 teaspoons olive oil
4 cups chicken or vegetable broth
2 cups water
⅔ cup uncooked brown rice
2 cups diced chicken or turkey, or 1 cup textured
    vegetable protein (TVP)
1 cup minced green cabbage
1 cup peas (fresh or frozen)
2 teaspoons Sea Veg Mix (page 56) or ¼ teaspoon
    kelp
½ teaspoon sea salt
1 bay leaf
¼ teaspoon powdered sage
½ teaspoon dried thyme
½ teaspoon ground ginger
½ teaspoon black pepper
¼ cup minced fresh parsley
2 teaspoons miso

Place onion, garlic, carrots, and oil in large soup pot.
Sauté 5 minutes, or until onions are soft. Add broth,
water, rice, poultry or TVP, cabbage, peas, sea vegetables, salt, bay leaf, sage, thyme, ginger, and
pepper. Cover and bring to a boil over high heat.
Reduce heat and simmer 45 minutes, or until rice is
soft. Remove from heat. Take out and discard bay leaf.
Stir in parsley and miso.

Yield: 6 to 8 servings

Note: This is a fortifying soup. It is especially good during cold and flu season. If your child is sick and doesn't want to eat, serve the broth in a cup. She'll still get the vitamins and minerals she needs. Cabbage and parsley are high in vitamin C. Sage and thyme help with stuffy noses and coughs.

Variation:

Cream of Chicken Soup

Puree cooked soup in blender or food processor for a smooth, creamy soup.

☺Tip: Never boil miso. The beneficial enzymes will be destroyed. After the soup or sauce is cooked, remove it from heat. Mix miso with a little water or soup broth to form a smooth paste. Then stir miso/liquid mixture into the soup or sauce. When reheating, do not boil.☺

Split Pea Soup

This hearty soup is perfect on a cold day.

> 1 cup dried split green peas
> ½ cup pearled or semi-hulled barley
> 1 bay leaf
> 2 quarts water
> 1 tablespoon Sea Veg Mix (page 56) or ½ teaspoon
>   kelp
> 1 teaspoon celery seed
> 1 onion, minced
> 2 carrots, diced
> 2 stalks celery, diced
> 2 medium white potatoes or 1 large sweet potato,
>   diced
> ½ cup minced collards, kale, chard, or other greens
> 1 teaspoon sea salt
> 2 teaspoons Bragg Liquid Aminos
> ½ teaspoon pepper
> ½ teaspoon dried basil
> ½ teaspoon dried thyme
> 2 tablespoons miso

Place split peas, barley, bay leaf, and water in large pot. Cover and bring to boil. Reduce heat and simmer for 1½ hours. Add remaining ingredients, except miso. Simmer for another 30 minutes, or until vegetables are soft. Remove from heat. Stir in miso.

Yield: 8 servings

Note: This soup thickens as it sits in the refrigerator because the barley absorbs the liquid. Add extra water if necessary when reheating. The thick consistency makes it easy for baby to eat.

Variation: Puree half or all of the soup for a creamy texture.

Lentil Stew

This stew is thick enough for baby to eat with her fingers.

> 1 cup dried lentils
> 1 cup brown rice
> ½ strip kombu
> 7 cups water
> 2 cups diced carrots, sweet potatoes, or winter squash
> 1 cup sliced green beans
> 1 cup minced kale, collards, chard, or cabbage
> 1 cup diced tomatoes with juice
> 1 tablespoon Bragg Liquid Aminos or low-sodium soy sauce
> 1 teaspoon dried basil
> 1 tablespoon miso

Place lentils, rice, kombu, and water in a large pot. Cover and bring to a boil. Reduce heat and simmer 25 minutes. Add carrots, potatoes or squash, and green beans. Cover and simmer 20 minutes, or until lentils are soft. Stir in remaining ingredients. Simmer 5 minutes. Top with shredded cheese, yogurt, or sour cream if desired.

Yield: 8 servings

Note: Here is a delicious way to use up leftover stew.

Lentil Bars

Let stew sit in the refrigerator overnight to thicken. Spread stew in an oiled baking pan. Bake at 400° for 30 minutes. Remove bars from oven and top with shredded cheese. Bake another 5 minutes, or until cheese is melted. Remove from oven. Wait 5 minutes before cutting to allow bars to set.

Sandwiches

Sandwiches made with two slices of bread and a filling are hard for little mouths to bite and tend to fall apart. Spread a thin layer of any of the following toppings on a slice of whole grain bread or toast. Cut the bread into "fingers" or quarters. These spreads are also good on crackers and rice cakes.

Bread and Cracker Toppings

- Almond butter, tahini, or peanut butter
- Cream, cottage, or ricotta cheese
- Olive or flax oil
- Mashed banana
- Mashed avocado
- Cooked squash or carrots mashed with olive oil
- Cooked beans mashed with olive oil
- Pureed tofu
- Fruit puree or fruit-sweetened jam
- Applesauce
- Hummus

☺Tip: Don't skimp on fat, especially when baby is weaning. Baby's brain develops most dramatically in the first two years and needs omega-3 and omega-6 essential fatty acids. Nuts, seeds, avocados, and olive oil contain beneficial fats.☺

Cheesy-Apple Toast

Spread a **slice of whole grain bread** with **olive or flax oil**. Cover with **grated apple** and top with a **slice of cheese**. Bake at 400° in a toaster oven for 2 minutes, or until cheese is melted.

Yield: 1 sandwich

Avocado and Nutritional Yeast Sandwich

My daughter Emily eats these sandwiches faster than I can make them.

Spread a **slice of whole grain bread or toast** with **mashed avocado**. Sprinkle with **nutritional yeast flakes**.

Yield: 1 sandwich

Almost Turkey Sandwich

My older daughter loves turkey-avocado sandwiches. The baby, of course, wanted what her big sister was eating. Hence, the creation of this meal.

1 slice whole grain bread
Olive oil or mayonnaise
1 slice turkey
¼ avocado

Spread a slice of whole grain bread or toast with olive oil or mayonnaise. Dice turkey, avocado, and bread. Serve as finger food.

Yield: 1 serving

Variation: For a vegetarian version, substitute diced tofu, tempeh, or cheese for turkey.

Grains and Vegetables

Millet-Quinoa

¼ cup millet
¼ cup quinoa
1 teaspoon Sea Veg Mix (page 56) or pinch kelp
1½ cups water
1 teaspoon olive or flax oil (optional)
1 tablespoon minced parsley

Place millet, quinoa, sea vegetables, and water in pan. Cover and bring to a boil over high heat. Reduce heat and simmer 25 minutes, or until water is absorbed. Mix in oil and parsley.

Yield: 1½ cups

Veggie-Rice Pilaf

My kids could eat rice at every meal. This dish ensures that they eat enough vegetables, too.

¾ cup brown rice
½ zucchini, diced or grated
1 small carrot, grated
¼ cup minced kale, collards, or other leafy greens
1 teaspoon Sea Veg Mix (page 56) or ¼ teaspoon
    kelp
2 cups water

Place all ingredients in pan. Cover and bring to a boil over high heat. Reduce heat and simmer 45 minutes, or until water is absorbed.

Yield: About 1¾ cups

☺Tip: Use leftover Veggie-Rice Pilaf to make Quick Cheesy Rice (page 58).☺

Sweet Potato Surprise

1 sweet potato, peeled and diced
½ cup chopped cauliflower
1 teaspoon nutritional yeast flakes
¼ teaspoon ground cinnamon or ginger
½ teaspoon olive or flax oil

Place sweet potato and cauliflower in pan with 1 inch of water. Cover and simmer over low heat until vegetables are soft. Drain vegetables and toss with remaining ingredients.

Yield: About 1½ cups

Carrots and Beets

2 carrots, diced
2 beets, diced
½ teaspoon olive or flax oil (optional)

Place carrots and beets in pan with 1 inch of water. Cover and simmer over low heat until vegetables are soft. Drain vegetables and toss with oil.

Yield: About 1 cup

Mashed Parsnips

3 parsnips, peeled and diced (about 2 cups)
½ teaspoon Sea Veg Mix (page 56) or pinch kelp
2 teaspoons minced parsley
Pinch ground nutmeg
1 teaspoon olive or flax oil

Place parsnips and sea vegetables in pan with 1 inch of water. Cover and simmer until parsnips are soft. Mash with remaining ingredients.

Yield: 1½ cups

Baby Cole Slaw

1 apple
2 carrots
2 cups chopped red or green cabbage
2 tablespoons orange or apple juice
¼ cup plain yogurt

In a food processor with metal blade, mince apple, carrots, and cabbage. Mix minced vegetables with juice and yogurt.

Yield: 4 to 6 servings

Variation: For a non-dairy salad, substitute ¼ cup mayonnaise or an additional 2 tablespoons juice for yogurt.

Sea Veg Mix

This mixture makes it easy to incorporate sea vegetables into your family's meals. It can be cooked with soup, grains, or vegetables.

2 tablespoons kelp
¼ cup crushed hiziki
¼ cup crushed arame
¼ cup crushed wakame
1 strip kombu

Crush the sea vegetables with your hands and place them in blender. Grind to a coarse powder. Store in covered jar.

Yield: ¾ cup

Entrées

Tahini-Millet and Veggies

½ cup millet or quinoa
1 carrot, minced
¼ cup minced cabbage
1 teaspoon Sea Veg Mix (page 56) or pinch kelp
1¾ cups water
1 tablespoon tahini

Place grain, carrot, cabbage, sea vegetables, and water in pan. Cover and bring to a boil over high heat. Reduce heat to low and simmer 25 minutes. Mix in tahini.

Yield: 2 cups

Quinoa and Egg

½ cup cooked quinoa
1 hard-boiled egg yolk or whole egg, chopped
1 teaspoon olive or flax oil
1 tablespoon minced parsley

Toss warm quinoa with egg, oil, and parsley.

Yield: 1 serving

Cooking Quinoa

Pour **1 cup quinoa** and **2½ cups water** in pan. Cover and bring to boil over high heat. Reduce heat to low. Simmer 15 to 20 minutes, or until water is absorbed.

Yield: 2½ cups

Quick Cheesy Rice

This dish is so easy to make with leftover rice. It's a favorite with all my children.

½ cup cooked brown rice
1 to 2 tablespoons shredded cheese
½ teaspoon olive or flax oil
1 tablespoon minced fresh parsley

Mix warm rice with cheese, oil, and parsley.

Yield: 1 serving

Cooking Brown Rice

Pour **1 cup brown rice** (long grain, short grain, or basmati) and **2 cups water** in pan. Cover and bring to boil over high heat. Reduce heat to low. Simmer 40 minutes, or until water is absorbed.

Yield: 2 cups

Rice and Beans

½ cup adzuki beans
½ cup brown rice
½ strip kombu
3 cups water
½ cup minced kale or collard greens

Place beans, rice, kombu, and water in pan. Cover and bring to boil over high heat. Reduce heat and simmer 60 minutes, or until beans are soft. Stir in greens. If desired, top with grated cheese or yogurt.

Yield: 2½ cups

Tofu and Noodles

4 cups cooked whole grain pasta noodles
8 ounces tofu, diced
1 medium zucchini, grated
2 teaspoons olive oil
¼ cup minced parsley
Sea salt
Black pepper

Sauté tofu and zucchini in a skillet with olive oil until tofu is slightly browned. Cover and steam mixture 10 minutes, or until zucchini is soft. Remove from heat. Stir in noodles and parsley. Add salt and pepper to taste. Add additional olive oil if desired.

Yield: 4 servings

Cooking Pasta

Bring **2 quarts water** to a boil in large pan. Stir **8 ounces pasta** into boiling water. Boil pasta 5 to 15 minutes, until tender but not mushy. Pour pasta into a colander to drain.

Yield: About 4 cups

Creamy Green Pasta

4 cups cooked whole grain pasta noodles
½ cup minced kale or other leafy greens
6 ounces cream, ricotta, or cottage cheese
¼ to ½ cup hot noodle-cooking water

Cook pasta as directed above. Drain, but reserve cooking water. Mash cheese with greens. Add hot noodle water a little at a time until mixture is soft and creamy. Gently toss cheese mixture with hot noodles.

Yield: 4 servings

Garbanzos and Avocado

When baby gets too old for mashed foods, use this as a spread on sandwiches or as a dip for veggies.

> ½ **cup cooked garbanzo beans (chick peas)**
> ½ **ripe avocado**
> **Pinch sea salt**

Mash or puree all ingredients together with a little bean-cooking water.

Yield: 2 servings

Note: You can buy canned garbanzo beans, or cook them yourself as follows.

Cooking Garbanzo Beans

Soak **1 cup beans** in **4 cups water** for 6 hours or overnight. Drain. Put beans into heavy pot with **4 cups water** and **1 strip kombu**. Cover and bring to boil. Reduce heat and simmer 2 to 3 hours, or until beans are tender.

Yield: 3 cups

Tempeh and Vegetables

> **2 ounces tempeh, diced**
> **1 cup diced winter squash**
> ½ **cup chopped cauliflower**
> ½ **teaspoon Sea Veg Mix (page 56) or pinch kelp**

Place all ingredients in pan with 1 inch of water. Cover and simmer over low heat 20 minutes, or until vegetables are soft. Serve chunky or mashed.

Yield: 2 servings

Tofu, Cauliflower, and Potato

1 medium potato, diced
½ cup chopped cauliflower
2 ounces tofu, diced
½ teaspoon Sea Veg Mix (page 56) or pinch kelp
1 teaspoon olive or flax oil

Place potato, cauliflower, tofu, and sea vegetables in pan with 1 inch of water. Cover and simmer 20 minutes, or until vegetables are soft. Drain and toss with oil.

Yield: 2 servings

Note: Never use green or sprouted potatoes. The poisonous alkaloids can be harmful to infants.

Baby Fish Dinner

Cold-water fish contain omega-3 essential fatty acids which are important for brain development.

¼ cup brown rice
½ teaspoon Sea Veg Mix (page 56)
¼ cup chopped green beans
3 ounces salmon or halibut, washed,
    boned, and chopped
1 cup vegetable or poultry broth, or water

Place all ingredients in pan. Cover and bring to a boil over high heat. Reduce heat and simmer 40 minutes. Serve chunky or mashed.

Yield: 1 to 2 servings

Variation: For a vegetarian meal, substitute tofu or tempeh for fish.

Chicken and Broccoli

1 medium potato, diced
½ cup chopped broccoli
¼ cup minced cooked chicken
½ teaspoon Sea Veg Mix (page 56) or pinch kelp

Place potato, broccoli, chicken, and sea vegetables in pan with 1 inch of water. Cover and simmer 20 minutes, or until vegetables are soft. Serve chunky or mashed.

Yield: 2 servings

Note: Never use green or sprouted potatoes. The poisonous alkaloids can be harmful to infants.

Ground Turkey and Veggies

4 ounces ground turkey
1 teaspoon olive oil
1 carrot, diced
½ cup peas
½ teaspoon Sea Veg Mix (page 56) or pinch kelp
½ cup water or vegetable broth

In medium-size pan, brown turkey in oil over low heat. Stir in carrot and peas. Add sea vegetables and liquid. Cover and bring to a boil over high heat. Reduce heat and simmer 15 minutes, or until vegetables are soft. Serve chunky or mashed.

Yield: 2 servings

Variation: For a vegetarian meal, use diced tempeh or soy ground beef substitute instead of ground turkey.

Finger Foods and Snacks

Encourage your baby to eat finger foods. At each meal, serve at least one thing baby can eat with her hands. It will help improve coordination and give you time to take a few bites of your own meal. If baby is crying for food and the meal is not quite ready, a few morsels on her tray will keep your child occupied while you finish cooking.

Continue to serve the finger foods suggested in the *Intermediate Foods* section. Here are more choices for the older baby.

Older Baby Finger Foods

- Chunks of firm tofu (raw or steamed)
- Chunks of steamed tempeh
- Chunks of hard-boiled egg yolk or whole egg
- Scrambled egg yolks or whole eggs
- Chunks of cheese
- Grated apple, pear, or carrot
- Cooked grains (cold, sticky chunks are easy for baby to pick up)
- Pretzels (made with no salt, sugar, or hydrogenated oils)
- Soft crackers (low salt, low sugar, and no hydrogenated oils)
- Leftover pancakes, french toast, or waffles

Sunflower-Oat Crackers

These wheat-free crackers contain protein, calcium, iron, and essential fatty acids.

1 cup hulled sunflower seeds
½ cup rolled oats
Pinch kelp
¼ cup water

Preheat oven to 300°. Oil a baking sheet. Grind seeds and oats to powder in food processor or blender. Place mixture in a bowl with remaining ingredients, and knead just until mixed. Place dough on prepared baking sheet. Roll dough out to ⅛-inch thickness. Score into squares, and prick with fork. Bake for 15 to 20 minutes, or until edges are golden. Let crackers cool before removing from pan.

Yield: 3 dozen

Teething Crackers

2 tablespoons molasses
2 tablespoons canola or safflower oil
1 egg yolk
1 teaspoon pure vanilla extract
Pinch kelp or sea salt
1 cup brown rice, barley, or whole wheat flour
1 to 2 tablespoons water or milk

Preheat oven to 350°. Blend molasses, oil, egg yolk, and vanilla. Stir in remaining ingredients to form a stiff dough. Add additional liquid if dough is too dry. Add extra flour if dough is too wet. On floured board, roll dough out to ¼-inch thickness. Score dough into 1 x 2-inch strips. Place strips on unoiled baking sheet. Bake 12 to 15 minutes, or until lightly browned.

Yield: 2 dozen

Apple-Bran Muffins

These moist, fruity muffins can be made without wheat.

3 tablespoons canola or safflower oil
3 tablespoons molasses
1 egg
1 cup plain yogurt
½ cup apple juice
1 cup whole wheat, brown rice, or barley flour
1 teaspoon baking soda
½ teaspoon ground cinnamon
1½ cups wheat or oat bran
¼ teaspoon sea salt
1 apple, grated
½ cup sunflower seeds or walnuts, minced

Preheat oven to 375°. Oil muffin tins. Beat together oil, molasses, egg, yogurt, and juice until smooth. In separate bowl, sift flour, baking soda, and cinnamon together. Stir in salt and bran. Mix yogurt mixture into flour mixture. Stir in apples and minced seeds or nuts. Pour batter into prepared muffin tins. Bake for 20 minutes, or until knife inserted in center comes out clean. Muffins keep well in refrigerator or freezer.

Yield: 1 dozen

Desserts

The longer you hold off introducing really sweet foods, the better. Babies will eat plain, unseasoned food because their taste buds haven't been corrupted. You may even want to limit fruits. Wait until after your baby has eaten a non-sweet food and give fruit for dessert.

Dessert Applesauce

½ cup unsweetened applesauce
Pinch ground cinnamon
1 teaspoon minced walnuts or almonds

Place applesauce in a small bowl. Sprinkle with cinnamon and minced nuts.

Yield: 1 serving

Squash Pudding

2 cups cooked winter squash or pumpkin
½ cup milk (dairy or non-dairy)
1 to 2 tablespoons brown rice syrup, maple syrup, honey, or molasses
½ teaspoon pure vanilla extract
1 teaspoon ground cinnamon or cardamom

Puree all ingredients together in food processor or blender. Chill. Serve plain, or with milk or yogurt.

Yield: 4 servings

Note: Use canned squash, or cook your own as shown on page 98.

Un-Jello

Agar Agar is a sea vegetable rich in vitamins and minerals. It is a soothing food, perfect for infants or sick children.

2 cups pure fruit juice
3 tablespoons agar agar flakes
1 cup sliced fruit (bananas, peaches, strawberries, etc.)

Place juice and agar agar in pan. Bring to boil. Reduce heat and simmer 5 minutes, or until flakes are dissolved. Remove from heat and stir in fruit. Pour Un-Jello into a serving bowl or mold, or individual-size bowls. Chill 1 hour, or until firm. Serve plain, with milk, or with a dollop of yogurt.

Yield: 4 servings

Cinnamon Noodles

My mom used to make this treat whenever we had leftover noodles. My children enjoy it as much as I did.

2 cups cooked pasta noodles, hot
1 tablespoon butter or olive oil
1 teaspoon ground cinnamon

Toss hot noodles with butter or oil and cinnamon until noodles are coated.

Yield: 4 servings

Note: Find instructions for cooking pasta on page 59.

☺Tip: To heat cold pasta, drop noodles in boiling water for 30 seconds. Drain.☺

Cakes, Bars, and Cookies

Pineapple-Carrot Cake

This is our favorite cake. It is moist and flavorful and just sweet enough. It's perfect for baby's first birthday. Use Ener-G Egg Replacer if baby is not eating eggs yet.

2 eggs, beaten
⅓ cup maple syrup, honey, or brown rice syrup
⅓ cup plain yogurt
¼ cup canola or safflower oil
1¾ cups crushed pineapple, drained
1½ cups grated carrots (about 3 carrots)
⅔ cup minced walnuts, almonds, or pecans
1½ cups whole wheat pastry flour
1 teaspoon baking powder
1 teaspoon baking soda
¾ teaspoon ground cinnamon
½ teaspoon ground ginger
¼ teaspoon ground nutmeg

Preheat oven to 300°. Oil a 9-inch springform pan. Beat together eggs, sweetener, yogurt, and oil until smooth. Stir in pineapple, carrots, and nuts. In separate bowl, sift together flour, baking powder, baking soda, cinnamon, ginger, and nutmeg. Stir flour mixture gently into carrot batter. Pour batter into prepared pan.

Bake 60 to 70 minutes, or until knife inserted in center of cake comes out clean. Frost cooled cake with Pineapple-Yogurt Frosting (recipe follows) or Cream Cheese Frosting (page 114).

Yield: 8 servings

Note: Crushed pineapple comes in 20-ounce cans containing approximately 2¼ cups pineapple. Save the remaining ½ cup pineapple to use in the frosting.

Pineapple-Yogurt Frosting

When the liquid or whey is drained from yogurt, it becomes firm like cream cheese. Mixed with fruit, you have an easy, sugar-free frosting.

16 ounces plain yogurt
½ cup crushed pineapple, drained
2 tablespoons unsweetened coconut flakes

Line a colander with several layers of cheesecloth. Place a dish underneath to catch drippings. Pour yogurt into center of colander. Let yogurt drain in refrigerator overnight.

Place yogurt cheese in bowl. Gently mix in the pineapple. Spread frosting over cooled cake. Sprinkle with coconut.

Yield: 2½ cups

Raisin Bars

These delicious bars contain no eggs or sweeteners.

1 cup whole wheat, brown rice, or barley flour
1 cup rolled oats
½ teaspoon sea salt
¼ cup canola or safflower oil
1 cup walnuts, minced
1 cup raisins, minced
1 cup pitted prunes, minced
1 tablespoon grated orange or lemon peel (optional)
⅓ to ½ cup water

Preheat oven to 325°. Oil 8-inch square baking pan. Blend flour, oats, salt, and oil with fingers until evenly mixed.

Mince the nuts in food processor and add to oat mixture. Mince raisins and prunes in food processor. Add them to batter along with the orange or lemon peel and *⅓ cup water*. Mix the batter with your hands or in food processor. Add remaining water as necessary to make batter hold together.

Press into prepared pan. Bake for 30 minutes. Let cool, and cut into 16 squares.

Yield: 16 bars

Banana-Oatmeal Cookies

These moist cookies contain no sweeteners, butter, eggs, or wheat.

2 cups rolled oats
⅔ cup almonds
1 teaspoon baking powder
¼ teaspoon sea salt
½ teaspoon ground cinnamon
¼ teaspoon ground nutmeg
1½ cups mashed banana (about 3 bananas)
¼ cup canola or safflower oil
1 teaspoon pure vanilla extract
¾ cup raisins

Preheat oven to 350°. Lightly oil baking sheet. Grind oats and almonds to a coarse powder in food processor or blender. Pour them into a large mixing bowl. Stir in baking powder, salt, cinnamon, and nutmeg.

In separate bowl or in food processor, beat together bananas, oil, and vanilla until smooth and creamy. Add banana mixture and raisins to oat mixture. Mix well.

Drop cookie dough by tablespoons onto prepared baking sheet. Bake for 13 to 16 minutes, or until bottoms are golden brown.

Yield: 3 dozen

Variation: For older children, replace the raisins with carob or chocolate chips if desired.

Beverages

Encourage your child to drink water. Give milk or juice sparingly. Dilute juice with water or milk to take the edge off the sweetness and lessen potential damage to teeth.

Babies can master sippy cups very early because they are used to sucking from the breast or bottle. If you are nursing, you can go straight from the breast to the cup and skip the bottle altogether. Never put baby to sleep with a bottle in her mouth, especially with juice. It can cause tooth decay.

Easy Soy Milk

Place **¼ cup tofu** and **⅔ cup water** in blender. Puree until smooth.

Yield: 1 to 2 servings

Banana Milk

1 banana, peeled and sliced
1 cup water

Place all ingredients in blender. Puree until smooth.

Yield: 1 to 2 servings

Almond Milk

Almonds are an excellent source of minerals, including calcium and iron. You can substitute almond milk for dairy or soy milk in any recipe.

½ cup raw almonds
2 cups water, or 1¼ cups water and ¾ cups apple juice

Grind almonds dry to a powder in blender. Add liquid and blend until smooth. Use *as is* in smoothies, cereals, or cooking. For a smooth drinking texture, pour milk through a fine strainer or cheesecloth. Nut pulp can be added to hot or cold cereal, or used as a facial scrub (for you, not baby!).

Yield: 2 cups

Pineapple and Almond Milk Shake-Up

½ cup pineapple juice
½ cup unsweetened Almond Milk (recipe above)

Pour juice and milk into a jar. Shake until blended.

Yield: 1 to 2 servings

Apple-Yogurt Shake-Up

½ cup unsweetened apple juice
½ cup plain yogurt

Pour juice and yogurt into a jar. Shake until blended.

Yield: 1 to 2 servings

Watermelon Cream

This is our favorite summer refresher.

2 cups cubed watermelon (seeds removed)
Pinch kelp
½ cup plain yogurt

Place ingredients in blender and puree until smooth.

Yield: 2 to 3 servings

☺Tip: Blended drinks may clog a sippy cup. Use a baby-straw cup instead.☺

Strawberry-Cashew Shake

Rich cashew nuts make a smooth, creamy shake.

¼ cup raw cashews
1 cup water
½ cup sliced fresh or frozen sweet strawberries

Grind cashews to powder in blender. Add water and fruit. Puree until smooth.

Yield: 2 servings

☺Tip: Find instructions for freezing fruit on page 111.☺

Peach-Almond Shake

¼ cup raw almonds
1 cup water
½ cup sliced fresh or frozen ripe peaches

Grind almonds to powder in blender. Add water and fruit. Puree until smooth.

Yield: 2 servings

Herbal Teas

The following herbal teas can comfort a sick, colicky, or teething baby. Infants can have these teas even if they're not ready for solid foods. In addition, the nursing mother may drink the tea and the benefits will pass to baby. Serve tea warm in a cup or bottle.

IMPORTANT NOTE
This is not intended as medical advice. Consult your pediatrician if baby is sick.

☺Tip: If child won't drink the tea, try 1 part apple juice to 2 parts tea.☺

Chamomile Tea

Chamomile calms and soothes a restless, irritable, teething, or colicky child. It also helps baby to sleep.

Place **1 teaspoon dried chamomile flowers or 1 tea bag** in heat-proof cup or jar. Pour **1 cup boiling water** over herbs. Steep for 5 minutes.

Yield: 1 to 2 servings

Fennel Tea

Fennel relieves gas, aids digestion, and calms a gassy or colicky baby.

Place **1 teaspoon fennel seeds or 1 tea bag** in heat-proof cup or jar. Pour **1 cup boiling water** over seeds. Steep for 10 to 15 minutes. Dilute with water if brew is very dark.

Yield: 1 to 2 servings

Catnip Tea

This tea calms and soothes a restless or colicky baby. It encourages sleep and helps prevent nightmares.

Place **1 teaspoon dried catnip leaves or 1 tea bag** in heat-proof cup or jar. Pour **1 cup boiling water** over herbs. Steep for 5 minutes.

Yield: 1 to 2 servings

Toddler

Foods

Fourteen Months and Up

Your child is now able to get around and feed himself. While most infants are willing to try new foods, many toddlers begin to develop definite food preferences and go through phases where they will eat only certain foods. I have incorporated fresh vegetables into many favorite dishes that wouldn't normally contain them, such as oatmeal, smoothies, and baked goods. In this way, even a finicky child will not miss out on the nutrients vegetables provide. All of the recipes in this section are suitable for the whole family, but special emphasis is placed on making the food easy for toddlers to eat by themselves.

☺Tip: Toddlers are not very helpful in the kitchen, though they want to be involved in what you are doing. With help, your toddler can sift flour, stir batter, and shape cookies. To occupy your child while you cook, give him a hunk of bread or cookie dough to roll and shape. Or give your toddler a mixing bowl and spoon so he can pretend to make his own concoctions. Play kitchens are a great place for your child to imitate you.☺

Breakfast Foods

Zucchini Oatmeal

It sounds strange, but this dish really is delicious. We eat it often in the summer since our garden always produces lots of zucchini. It's a great way to get an extra serving of vegetables.

**1 cup rolled oats
1 small apple, grated
½ medium zucchini, grated
¼ cup raisins
½ teaspoon cinnamon
1 teaspoon Sea Veg Mix (page 56) or pinch kelp
3 cups water**

Mix all ingredients in a pan. Bring to a boil over medium heat. Reduce heat to low. Simmer uncovered 15 minutes. Stir occasionally to prevent cereal from sticking to bottom of pan. Add water or milk if necessary for a thinner texture.

Yield: 4 servings

Serving Suggestion: Top cereal with milk or amasake and ground nuts or seeds if desired.

Breakfast Rice Pudding

Kids think it's a special treat to have a dessert food for breakfast.

> **2 cups cooked brown rice (page 58)**
> **1 cup milk (dairy or non-dairy)**
> **½ teaspoon pure vanilla extract**
> **¼ teaspoon ground nutmeg**
> **1 banana, diced**
> **½ cup walnuts, chopped**

Place rice, milk, vanilla, and nutmeg in pan. Warm over low heat. Stir in remaining ingredients and serve.

Yield: 4 servings

French Toast

> **2 eggs**
> **½ cup milk (dairy or non-dairy)**
> **¼ teaspoon ground cinnamon**
> **½ teaspoon pure vanilla extract**
> **5 to 6 slices whole grain bread**
> **Canola or safflower oil**

Beat together eggs, milk, cinnamon, and vanilla. Pour into shallow dish.

Warm skillet over medium heat. Pour a little oil into the skillet, and tilt pan from side to side to coat bottom. Dip bread into egg mixture, coating both sides. Place bread in hot skillet. Cook each side of bread 5 minutes, or until golden brown.

Serve with applesauce, unsweetened jam, chopped fresh fruit, and/or yogurt if desired. Baby will even love the toast plain.

Yield: 5 to 6 slices

Whole Grain Waffles

The yogurt, milk, and sesame seeds in this recipe add protein and calcium. These waffles can be made without wheat flour.

2 cups whole wheat, brown rice, or barley flour
2 teaspoons baking powder
1½ teaspoons baking soda
¼ cup sesame seeds
2 eggs, separated
1 tablespoon molasses, brown rice syrup, or honey
2 tablespoons oil
1 cup yogurt
1 cup milk

Sift flour, baking powder, and baking soda together. Mix in sesame seeds. In separate bowl, beat egg yolks, sweetener, oil, yogurt, and milk until smooth. Add yogurt mixture to dry ingredients and mix well. In separate bowl, beat egg whites until stiff. Fold egg whites gently into batter.

Heat waffle iron. Brush or spray cooking surfaces with oil. Pour in just enough batter to fill iron. Close iron, and bake until waffles are crisp on both sides. Top with fresh fruit and yogurt, or applesauce. Infants can eat waffles without toppings.

Yield: 6 waffles

Note: You may use *Ener-G Egg Replacer* instead of eggs. Add the equivalent of two eggs to the batter instead of the egg yolks. Ignore the instructions pertaining to egg whites.

Scrambled Tofu

2 teaspoons olive oil
8 ounces firm tofu
½ cup minced kale, collards, or broccoli
¼ teaspoon turmeric
1 teaspoon nutritional yeast flakes
1 teaspoon Bragg Liquid Aminos
¼ teaspoon black pepper
1 tablespoon water
¼ cup minced parsley

Pour olive oil into hot skillet. Crumble tofu with your hands, and add it to skillet. Stir in chopped greens. Cover and steam 5 minutes. Mix in seasonings and water. Cook and stir 5 minutes, or until tofu is uniformly yellow and heated through. Serve with whole grain toast or english muffin, if desired.

Yield: 2 to 3 servings

☺Tip: Scrambled Tofu tastes great in pita pockets.☺

Cinnamon Toast

Spread a **slice of whole grain toast** with **olive oil, flax oil, or butter**. Sprinkle with **ground cinnamon**.

Yield: 1 serving

Soups

Creamy Carrot Soup

My daughter calls this "Smoothie Soup" since it is finished in the blender. She likes to drink it warm out of a cup. This soup is delicious with a sandwich or toast.

1 pound carrots, cut into thick slices (about 3½ cups)
1 clove garlic, chopped
¼ onion, chopped
1 teaspoon Sea Veg Mix (page 56) or ¼ strip kombu
3 cups water
2 teaspoons Bragg Liquid Aminos
1 tablespoon tahini or peanut butter
2 teaspoons miso
4 ounces tofu (optional)
1 tablespoon minced fresh dill or 1 teaspoon dried
¼ cup minced parsley

Place carrots, garlic, onion, sea vegetables, and water in medium-size pan. Cover and bring to a boil over high heat. Reduce heat and simmer 15 to 20 minutes, or until carrots are tender.

In blender or food processor, puree cooked vegetables with remaining ingredients until completely smooth. (You will need to do this in two batches.)

Serve immediately or reheat later over low heat. Be careful not to boil when reheating as this will kill the enzymes in the miso.

Yield: 4 servings

Minestrone Soup

Almost any combination of vegetables can be used in this soup. Use whatever your children like best.

1 medium onion, minced
1 clove garlic, minced
1 stalk celery, minced
2 teaspoons olive oil
1 teaspoon dried basil
1 teaspoon dried oregano
½ teaspoon fennel seeds
1 bay leaf
6 cups vegetable stock or water
¼ cup crushed hiziki
1 large carrot, diced
1 cup sliced green beans (½-inch pieces)
½ cup chopped cauliflower
½ cup corn kernels (fresh or frozen)
4 cups diced tomatoes (fresh or canned) with juice
2 cups cooked adzuki beans (see next page)
½ cup minced kale, collards, or other leafy greens
½ cup minced fresh parsley
1½ teaspoons sea salt
½ teaspoon black pepper
8 ounces whole grain pasta noodles (uncooked)
1 tablespoon miso

Place onion, garlic, celery, and oil in large soup pot. Sauté vegetables 5 to 10 minutes over low heat, or until they are soft. Stir in basil, oregano, fennel, and bay leaf. Add water, hiziki, carrots, green beans, and cauliflower. Cover and bring to a boil over high heat. Reduce heat and simmer 20 minutes, or until vegetables are soft. Add corn, tomatoes, cooked adzuki beans, greens, parsley, salt, black pepper, and noodles. Simmer 5 to 10 minutes, or until pasta is tender but not mushy. Remove from heat. Stir in miso. Serve with grated parmesean cheese if desired.

Yield: 8 to 10 servings

Note: Cook your own adzuki beans as follows, or use canned beans. Kidney or pinto beans also work well in this soup.

Cooking Adzuki Beans

Place **1 cup adzuki beans**, **4 cups water**, and **½ strip kombu** in heavy pan. Cover and bring to boil over high heat. Reduce heat and simmer 50 minutes, or until beans are tender.

Yield: About 2½ cups

☺Tip: Freeze leftover soup in individual-size containers for a quick meal.☺

White Bean and Corn Chowder

*I serve this dairy-free soup often for family and friends.
It always receives compliments.*

½ onion, minced
2 teaspoons olive oil
1 clove garlic, minced
2 carrots, diced
2 medium red or white new potatoes, diced
4 cups water
1 bay leaf
1 teaspoon Sea Veg Mix (page 56) or pinch kelp
3¾ cup cooked white beans (see note below)
1 cup corn kernels (fresh or frozen)
1 teaspoon sea salt
Black pepper to taste
¼ cup minced fresh parsley
1 tablespoon nutritional yeast flakes
1 tablespoon miso

In large soup pot, sauté onions in oil until soft. Stir in garlic, carrots, and potatoes. Sauté 5 minutes. Add water, bay leaf, and sea vegetables. Cover and bring to boil. Reduce heat to low and simmer 20 minutes, or until vegetables are tender but not mushy. Add beans with liquid, corn, salt, and black pepper. Simmer 5 minutes, or until all ingredients are heated through. Remove from heat. Remove and discard bay leaf. Stir in parsley, nutritional yeast flakes, and miso.

Yield: 6 to 8 servings

Note: Use 2 (15-ounce) cans white beans, or cook your own as follows.

Cooking White Beans

Soak **1½ cup beans** in **4 cups water** for 6 hours or overnight. Drain. Put beans into heavy pot with **4½ cups water** and **1 strip kombu**. Cover and bring to boil. Reduce heat and simmer one hour, or until beans are tender.

Yield: About 3¾ cups

Potato-Kale Soup

We call this dish "Hotdog Soup". Kids love the creamy potatoes and veggie dog chunks. They won't even notice the kale.

6 medium potatoes, diced
2 cloves garlic, minced
2 stalks celery, diced
1 teaspoon salt
½ teaspoon kelp
1 bay leaf
4 cups water or vegetable broth
4 Tofu Pups or other vegetarian hot dogs, sliced
½ cup minced kale
1 tablespoon nutritional yeast
½ cup powdered milk (dairy or soy)
¾ teaspoon black pepper
1 tablespoon miso

Place potatoes, garlic, celery, salt, kelp, and bay leaf in large pot with water or broth. Cover and bring to a boil over high heat. Reduce heat and simmer 30 minutes, or until potatoes are tender. Mash or puree potato mixture until smooth. Add hot dogs, kale, nutritional yeast, milk powder, and pepper. Simmer 5 minutes. Remove from heat. Stir in miso.

Yield: 6 servings

Sandwiches

Cheesecake Sandwich

Spread **1 slice whole grain bread or toast** with **ricotta, cottage, or cream cheese**. Spread **second slice** with **mashed fruit or fruit-sweetened jam**. Place slices together, and cut into quarters.

Yield: 1 sandwich

Almond Butter-Applesauce Sandwich

Spread **1 slice whole grain bread or toast** with **almond or peanut butter**. Spread **second slice** with **applesauce** and sprinkle lightly with **ground cinnamon**. Place slices together, and cut into quarters.

Yield: 1 sandwich

Avocado and Carrot Sandwich

Grate ½ **carrot**. Mash with ½ **avocado**. Spread mixture on **1 slice whole grain bread or toast**. Spread **second slice** with **mayonnaise or cream cheese**. Place slices together, and cut into quarters.

Yield: 1 sandwich

Tahini-Banana Sandwich

Spread **1 slice whole grain bread or toast** with **tahini.**
Spread **second slice** with **mashed banana.** Place slices
together, and cut into quarters.

Yield: 1 sandwich

Egg or Tofu Salad

*I like fresh parsley in my egg salad but after several
experiences with visiting children who didn't like "green
things" in their sandwiches, I substituted cabbage.
When minced, it's virtually invisible. The cabbage,
carrots, and kelp add vitamins and minerals. Now the
kids gobble it up!*

1 stalk celery, minced
1 carrot, minced or grated
¼ cup minced green cabbage
8 hard-boiled eggs, peeled, or 12 ounces firm tofu
¼ teaspoon kelp
½ teaspoon sea salt
½ teaspoon black pepper
¼ cup mayonnaise

Mince celery, carrot, and cabbage in food processor
with metal blade. Slice eggs or tofu, and add to
vegetables in food processor. Add kelp, salt, black
pepper, and mayonnaise. Pulse to mix. Spread salad
between slices of bread, or stuff it in a pita pocket.

Yield: 6 servings

Bean and Cheese Pizzas

A fun lunch with lots of calcium and protein.

4 small whole wheat or corn tortillas
½ cup Bean Spread (recipe follows)
1 large tomato, diced
2 ounces jack or mozzarella cheese, shredded

Preheat oven to 400°. Place tortillas on baking sheet and spread them with Bean Spread. Arrange tomatoes on tortillas, and sprinkle with cheese. Bake 3 to 5 minutes, or until cheese is melted. Cut into wedges.

Yield: 4 servings

Bean Spread

2 cups cooked pinto beans
1 teaspoon olive oil
¼ teaspoon ground cumin
2 teaspoons nutritional yeast flakes
2 tablespoons fresh minced parsley or cilantro
¼ teaspoon sea salt

Puree or mash all ingredients together.

Yield: 1 cup

Note: Use canned beans, or cook your own as follows.

Cooking Pinto Beans

Soak **1 cup pinto beans** in **4 cups water** for 6 hours or overnight. Drain. Put beans into heavy pan with **3 cups water** and **1 strip kombu**. Cover and bring to boil. Reduce heat and simmer 1½ hours, or until beans are tender.

Yield: 2 cups

Grains and Vegetables

Tabouli for Tots

Your kids will love this alternative to traditional tabouli.

2¼ cups water
1 cup bulgur wheat
¼ teaspoon kelp
1 stalk celery, minced
1 carrot, grated or minced
½ cup minced cabbage
¼ cup toasted sunflower seeds
½ cup dried cranberries or currants
1½ cups packed fresh parsley, minced
3 tablespoons minced fresh mint leaves (optional)
¼ cup orange juice (about 1 orange)
2 tablespoons lemon juice (½ lemon)
¼ cup olive oil
Salt and pepper to taste

Bring water to a boil in medium-size pan. Add bulgur and kelp. Cover and return to boil. Remove from heat. Let bulgur sit covered for 20 to 30 minutes, or until water is absorbed. Mix in remaining ingredients. Refrigerate at least one hour before serving. Serve alone or in a pita pocket.

Yield: 4 to 6 servings

☺Tip: Parsley is a nutritious herb. Mince fresh parsley in your food processor and add it to baby's food. Freeze extra minced parsley so you'll always have some on hand.☺

Arame and Quinoa

Arame is rich in minerals, as well as vitamins and protein. Crumble it up, and your child will hardly notice it. Sea vegetables are especially beneficial for the child who won't eat fresh vegetables.

1 cup quinoa
¼ cup crushed arame
2½ cups water

Place quinoa, arame, and water in pan. Cover and bring to boil over high heat. Reduce heat to low. Simmer 20 minutes, or until water is absorbed. Remove from heat. Let stand covered for 5 minutes.

Yield: 4 servings

Sesame Rice

1½ cups brown rice
3 cups water
1 teaspoon Sea Veg Mix (page 56) or pinch kelp
2 teaspoons toasted sesame oil
2 tablespoons sesame seeds (raw or toasted)

Place rice, Sea Veg Mix, and water in pan. Cover and bring to boil. Reduce heat and simmer 40 minutes, or until water is absorbed. Stir in remaining ingredients.

Yield: 6 servings

Mashies

If you use red or new potatoes for this dish, you won't have to peel them.

4 medium potatoes
4 large carrots
1 bay leaf
½ strip kombu or 1 teaspoon Sea Veg Mix (page 56)
1 tablespoon miso
1 tablespoon nutritional yeast flakes
1 tablespoon olive or flax oil
½ teaspoon black pepper
¼ cup minced parsley
1 teaspoon dried thyme (or 1 tablespoon fresh)
2 tablespoons cooking water or milk

Scrub or peel potatoes and carrots, and cut into chunks. Place vegetables in pot with bay leaf and sea vegetables. Add 1 inch of water. Cover and bring to a boil over high heat. Reduce heat to low and simmer until vegetables are tender. Drain, but reserve cooking water if desired. Return vegetables to pot. Add miso, nutritional yeast, oil, black pepper, parsley, thyme, and 2 tablespoons cooking water or milk. Mash to desired consistency.

Yield: 6 servings

Note: Leftover potato-cooking water makes great soup stock.

Quick Zucchini and Carrots

These vegetables are the perfect size for little fingers.

2 carrots, grated
2 small zucchini, grated
2 teaspoons olive oil
2 teaspoons Bragg Liquid Aminos or low-sodium soy
   sauce
¼ cup minced fresh parsley

Stir carrots, zucchini, and oil together in skillet over low heat. Cover and steam vegetables 10 to 15 minutes, or until vegetables are soft. Stir in Aminos or soy sauce and parsley.

Yield: 6 servings

☺Tip: Use a food processor with the grating attachment to make uniform, attractive pieces of carrot and zucchini in seconds.☺

Brussels Spouts with Crumb Topping

My siblings and I used to fight over brussels sprouts when my mom made this crumb topping.

2 pounds brussels sprouts
2 tablespoons olive oil or butter
½ cup breadcrumbs

Trim stems from brussels sprouts, and cut large sprouts in half. Steam brussels sprouts over boiling water until tender. In small pan, warm olive oil or butter. Mix in breadcrumbs. Crumble over vegetables.

Yield: 4 to 6 servings

Entrées

Squash-Millet Balls

1 cup cooked winter squash
2 cups cooked millet (see next page)
2 teaspoons Bragg Liquid Aminos or low-sodium soy
  sauce
1 tablespoon miso
1 tablespoon nutritional yeast flakes
2 tablespoons minced fresh parsley
½ cup sesame seeds

Preheat oven to 375°. Oil baking sheet. In a large bowl, mix squash, millet, Bragg Liquid Aminos or soy sauce, miso, nutritional yeast flakes, and parsley with your hands. If mixture is too wet, add rolled oats. Shape mixture into 1-inch balls, and roll them in sesame seeds. Place balls on prepared baking sheet. Bake 20 to 25 minutes, turning balls once, until golden brown. Serve with Tahini Dipping Sauce (recipe follows).

Yield: 3 dozen

Note: Used canned squash or, for better flavor, bake your own. (See instructions on page 98.)

Tahini Dipping Sauce

¼ cup tahini, almond butter, or peanut butter
½ cup water
1 teaspoon Bragg Liquid Aminos or low-sodium soy
  sauce

Stir all ingredients together until smooth.

Yield: ¾ cup

Cooking Millet

Pour **1 cup millet** and **3 cups water** in pan. Cover and bring to boil over high heat. Reduce heat and simmer 20 to 25 minutes, or until water is absorbed.

Yield: 3½ cups

Baby Stir-Fry

The vegetables are well-cooked for easy chewing.

1½ cups brown rice
1 carrot, diced
1 teaspoon Sea Veg Mix (page 56)
3 cups water
1 cup minced greens
1 cup peas
2 teaspoons sesame oil
8 ounces firm tofu, cut into cubes
1 cup red or green seedless grapes, halved
¼ cup unsweetened pineapple or orange juice
2 teaspoons Bragg Liquid Aminos or low-sodium soy
    sauce
2 tablespoons sesame seeds

Place rice, carrot, Sea Veg Mix, and water in pan. Cover and bring to a boil over high heat. Reduce heat and simmer 35 minutes, or until water is absorbed. Stir in minced greens and peas.

Place oil and tofu in a large skillet or wok. Sauté over medium heat until tofu is golden brown. Reduce heat to low. Add cooked rice mixture and grapes. Stir gently to evenly distribute tofu and grapes throughout rice. Mix juice with Aminos or soy sauce, and pour over ingredients in skillet. Sprinkle with sesame seeds. Cook 5 minutes, or until sauce is hot.

Yield: 6 servings

Squashed Macaroni

This sweet, creamy sauce is made from winter squash—a good source of vitamin A. The tahini, parsley, and kelp add calcium. It's a nutritious alternative to cheese or tomato sauce.

2 cups cooked winter squash (butternut, hubbard, pumpkin, etc.)
1½ cups milk (dairy or non-dairy)
1 tablespoon miso
2 tablespoons tahini
1 tablespoon nutritional yeast flakes
½ teaspoon sea salt
Black pepper to taste
¼ teaspoon ground nutmeg
¼ cup minced fresh parsley
1 pound whole grain elbow macaroni, cooked
½ cup walnuts, minced

Puree squash, milk, miso, tahini, nutritional yeast, salt, pepper, nutmeg, and parsley in blender or food processor until smooth. Pour sauce into medium-size pan, and warm over low heat while pasta cooks.

Toss hot sauce gently with hot pasta until evenly mixed. Pour into a serving bowl. Sprinkle minced walnuts evenly over the top.

Yield: 6 to 8 servings

Note: Canned or frozen squash may be used, but it is easy to cook fresh squash as follows.

Baking Winter Squash

Preheat oven to 375°. Cut squash in half. Scrape out and discard seeds and pulp. Place squash, cut side down, on lightly oiled baking sheet. Add ¼ inch of water to pan. Bake 30 to 60 minutes, depending on size of squash. Squash will be easily pierced with a fork when done. Scoop out cooked squash.

Yield: 1 cup cooked squash per 1 pound of fresh

Almond Butter Noodles

**1 pound brown rice or whole wheat linguine,
  cooked (page 59)
2 teaspoons toasted sesame oil
3 carrots, grated (about 1 cup)
2 cups finely chopped green cabbage
1 cup peas (fresh or frozen)
¼ cup almond or peanut butter
¾ cup water
1 tablespoons Bragg Liquid Aminos or low-sodium
  soy sauce
½ teaspoon ground ginger**

While pasta is cooking, place oil, carrots, and cabbage in skillet. Sauté over medium-low heat for 5 minutes. Cover and steam 15 minutes, or until vegetables are soft. Stir in cooked pasta and peas. Whisk together nut butter, water, Bragg Liquid Aminos, and ginger. Pour over rice mixture. Heat 5 to 10 minutes, or until rice and peas are hot.

Yield: 4 to 6 servings

Quick Franks and Beans

Try these with Carrot-Corn Muffins (page 107).

4 Tofu Pups (or other vegetarian hot dogs), cooked and sliced
3¾ cups cooked white beans, with cooking water
¼ cup fruit-sweetened ketchup
½ teaspoon mustard powder
1 tablespoon nutritional yeast flakes
½ teaspoon sea salt
1 teaspoon Bragg Liquid Aminos or low-sodium soy sauce
¼ cup minced fresh parsley

Cook vegetarian hot dogs according to package directions. Meanwhile, drain beans, but reserve ⅔ cup cooking water. Place beans in pan. In small bowl, mix reserved bean water, ketchup, mustard powder, nutritional yeast, salt, and Bragg Liquid Aminos or soy sauce together until smooth. Pour sauce over beans. Stir in parsley and sliced franks. Warm over low heat to desired temperature.

Yield: 4 servings

Note: Use 2 (15-ounce) cans white beans, or cook your own as shown on page 87.

Tofu "Fish" Sticks

This is a big hit with kids of all ages!

1 pound firm tofu
½ cup fine bread or cracker crumbs
3 tablespoons sesame seeds
1 tablespoon nutritional yeast
¼ teaspoon paprika
½ teaspoon powdered kelp
3 tablespoons olive oil or 1 egg, beaten

Place tofu in shallow pan. Press out water by placing a weighted cutting board on tofu. Let tofu sit 15 to 30 minutes. Drain water.

In a pie plate or shallow bowl, combine crumbs, seeds, nutritional yeast flakes, paprika, and kelp.

Turn block of tofu on its side, and cut tofu in half lengthwise. Turn tofu back to widest side, and cut tofu into ½-inch slices across shorter end. You should have 12 pieces.

Preheat oven to 375°. Oil baking sheet. Pour olive oil or beaten egg into a shallow dish. Place tofu in oil or egg, and turn to coat all sides. Next, carefully roll sticks in breading mixture until coated.

Place breaded tofu sticks on prepared baking sheet. Bake 20 to 25 minutes, turning once, or until brown and crisp. Serve with tartar sauce for dipping.

Yield: 4 servings

Note: Buy all-natural tartar sauce, or make your own as follows.

Easy Tartar Sauce

¼ cup mayonnaise
2 tablespoons sweet pickle relish or chopped sweet
pickles

Mix mayonnaise and pickles together. Keep refrigerated until ready to serve.

Yield: ¼ cup

☺Tip: If you don't eat eggs, check your natural food store for an egg-free or soy mayonnaise.☺

Sesame Tempeh Fingers

1 to 2 tablespoons lemon juice (½ lemon)
1 tablespoon miso
1 tablespoon Bragg Liquid Aminos or low-sodium soy
sauce
1 tablespoon tahini
1 clove garlic, crushed
1 tablespoon minced fresh ginger or ½ teaspoon
ground ginger
8 ounces tempeh
2 tablespoons sesame seeds

Whisk together lemon juice, miso, Aminos or soy sauce, tahini, garlic, and ginger. Cut tempeh into ½-inch slices. Place tempeh in sauce, and mix gently until coated on all sides. Let tempeh marinate 15 minutes to 1 hour.

Preheat oven to 350°. Pour tempeh and sauce into baking dish, and arrange tempeh in single layer. Sprinkle sesame seeds over tempeh. Bake 20 to 25 minutes, or until tempeh is heated through.

Yield: 4 servings

Poached Fish

1 pound salmon, halibut, or other firm fish fillet or steak
Boiling water
3 to 4 tablespoons lemon juice (1 lemon)
2 tablespoons water
1 bay leaf
½ teaspoon kelp or sea salt
1 teaspoon dried dill

Cut fish into serving-size pieces and place in skillet. Cover fish with boiling water. Add remaining ingredients. Cover and simmer over low heat 5 to 10 minutes, or until fish is tender and cooked through. Carefully remove fish from water. Remove all bones and chop fish for baby.

Yield: 4 servings

☺Tip: Overcooked fish can be tough. Cut into thickest part of fish—it is done if it is opaque.☺

One-Pot Stuffing Dinner

This is a complete meal made in one pot with lots of chunks for baby to eat with his fingers. Try serving it with apple or cranberry sauce on the side.

½ medium onion, chopped
2 stalks celery, diced
2 teaspoons olive oil
2 cups poultry or vegetable broth
1½ cups water
1 teaspoon Sea Veg Mix (page 56) or pinch kelp
1 cup bulgur, millet, or quinoa
2 carrots, diced
1 apple, peeled, cored, and diced
1 cup chopped broccoli
1 cup diced cooked chicken, turkey, tempeh, or tofu
¼ teaspoon dried sage
½ teaspoon dried thyme
½ teaspoon sea salt
½ teaspoon black pepper

In large pan, sauté onion and celery in oil for 5 to 10 minutes, or until onion is soft. Add stock, water, and sea vegetables. Bring to boil over high heat. Add remaining ingredients. Cover and return to boil. Reduce heat and simmer 20 minutes. Remove from heat. Let sit covered 5 minutes before serving.

Yield: 4 servings

Note: You may substitute 2 tablespoons vegetarian chicken-flavored broth powder (available at natural food stores) and 2 cups water for broth.

Snacks

Toddlers need extra calories, but their small stomachs cannot hold much food. Three meals a day are not enough for all the energy they are using. Constant snacking can be damaging to teeth and leave your child too full to eat regular meals. Establish a morning and afternoon snack time. Avoid giving sugary or salty snacks as they tend to encourage overeating.

Healthful Snack Ideas

- Fresh fruit, plain or with yogurt for dipping
- Raw or steamed vegetables with hummus or salad dressing for dipping
- Unsweetened yogurt or cottage cheese with chopped fruit or applesauce
- Hot or cold cereals
- Leftover pancakes, french toast, or waffles with almond or apple butter
- Chunks of cheese with fruit or crackers
- Slices of avocado
- Diced tofu, tempeh, turkey, or chicken
- Hard-boiled egg slices
- Whole grain crackers, rice cakes, or rye crispbreads with almond, sesame, or peanut butter
- Bagels, english muffins, or toast with cream cheese or almond butter
- Pretzels (low-sodium and no hydrogenated oils)
- Sandwiches
- Smoothies
- Homemade popsicles
- Low-sugar, whole grain muffins or cookies

Animal Crackers

Your toddler will enjoy cutting these out with you.

½ cup apple juice
3 tablespoons canola or safflower oil
1 egg
1½ teaspoons pure vanilla extract
½ teaspoon sea salt
2 cups whole wheat, brown rice, or barley flour

Preheat oven to 350°. Beat together juice, oil, egg, and vanilla until smooth. Stir in remaining ingredients to form a stiff dough. Add additional juice if dough is too dry. Add extra flour if dough is too wet.
On floured board, roll dough out to ¼-inch thickness. Cut dough with animal-shaped cookie cutters. Place on unoiled baking sheet. Bake 12 to 15 minutes, or until lightly browned.

Yield: About 4 dozen

Note: For quick preparation, cut crackers into squares and bake as directed.

Graham Crackers

¼ cup almond or peanut butter
¼ cup canola or safflower oil
1 tablespoon honey
1 tablespoon molasses
1 teaspoon pure vanilla extract
½ cup milk (dairy or non-dairy)
1 cup whole wheat flour
1 cup whole wheat pastry flour
½ teaspoon baking powder

Preheat oven to 400°. Oil two baking sheets. Beat together peanut butter, oil, honey, molasses, and vanilla until smooth. Beat in milk. Mix together flours and baking powder. Add wet ingredients to dry, and knead just until mixed.

Divide dough in half. Roll each half to ⅛-inch thickness on prepared baking sheet. Score into squares. Prick with fork. Bake 6 to 8 minutes, or until edges are brown. Cool completely. Store in airtight container.

Yield: About 4 dozen

Variation:

Cinnamon Graham Crackers

Add 1 teaspoon ground cinnamon to dry ingredients, and prepare as directed above.

Carrot-Corn Muffins

These colorful, wheat-free muffins go great with soup. We like them for breakfast with orange marmalade.

1 cup plain yogurt
½ cup milk (dairy or non-dairy)
2 eggs
1 tablespoon honey or maple syrup
1 tablespoon canola or safflower oil
2¼ cups cornmeal
½ teaspoon baking soda
1 teaspoon baking powder
½ teaspoon sea salt
1 cup grated carrots (2 to 3 carrots)

Preheat oven to 375°. Oil baking tins. Beat together yogurt, milk, eggs, sweetener, and oil until smooth. In separate bowl, whisk together cornmeal, baking soda, baking powder, and salt. Add yogurt mixture and carrots to cornmeal mixture. Stir just until mixed. Pour into prepared baking tins. Bake for 20 minutes, or until a knife inserted in center comes out dry.

Yield: 1 dozen

Note: 1½ cups buttermilk may be substituted for yogurt and milk.

Variation:
Carrot-Corn Bread

Pour batter into an oiled 9-inch square baking pan or 10-inch cast iron skillet. Bake 45 minutes, or until knife inserted in center comes out clean.

Whole Grain-Sesame Pretzels

Let your toddler help shape these soft pretzels.

2 cups whole wheat or rye flour
1 teaspoon active dry yeast
¾ teaspoon sea salt
¾ cup milk (dairy or non-dairy)
1 tablespoon honey or brown rice syrup
2 quarts boiling water
2 tablespoons salt
¼ cup sesame seeds

In large bowl, mix *1 cup* of the flour with yeast and salt. Heat milk and honey over low heat until warm but not hot and add to flour mixture. Beat vigorously for 3 minutes. Stir in remaining flour. On wet surface with wet hands, knead dough for approximately 8 minutes, or until dough is smooth and elastic. Keep surface and hands wet enough to prevent dough from sticking. Form dough into ball. Place in a lightly oiled bowl. Cover with a damp cloth and let dough rise in a warm place for one hour, or until doubled in size.

Press down dough. Divide it into 16 equal parts. Roll pieces into 12-inch long ropes. To form pretzels, shape each rope into a circle with ends overlapping 3 inches. Twist strands where circle joins. Bring overlaps to opposite end, and tuck them under edge. Press to seal. Place pretzels on floured board. Cover with damp cloth and let rise 20 minutes. Meanwhile, bring 2 quarts of water to a boil in large pot.

Preheat oven to 350°. Oil large baking sheet. Dissolve salt in water. Lower 3 pretzels at a time into boiling water. After 45 seconds, remove pretzels from water with a slotted spoon. Place them on prepared baking sheet. Sprinkle with sesame seeds.

Bake 15 minutes, or until golden brown. Remove from baking sheet, and cool on wire rack.

Yield: 16

Desserts

Instant Banana Pudding

This luscious dessert takes just minutes to make.

2 tablespoons milk (dairy or non-dairy)
1 teaspoon lemon juice
½ teaspoon pure vanilla extract
8 ounces firm or silken tofu, cut into chunks
2 medium bananas, sliced (about 1¾ cups)
1½ tablespoons tahini
Pinch ground nutmeg

Place all ingredients in a food processor or blender, and puree until smooth. Chill. Top with chopped nuts if desired.

Yield: 4 servings

Note: Since there is not much liquid, it can be hard to get your puree going in a blender. Put the liquids in first, and cut the tofu and banana into small pieces. Don't add additional liquid or pudding will be soupy.

Variations:

Peanut Butter-Banana Pudding

Substitute peanut (or almond) butter for tahini.

Carob-Banana Pudding

Add 2 teaspoons carob powder and puree with other ingredients.

Better Than Ice Cream

Even babies love ice cream, but they don't need all that sugar. This frozen treat whips up in seconds, and you won't believe how good it tastes. You may add sweetener if you like, but I haven't found it necessary.

☺Tip: These also make great popsicles. Just pour into molds and freeze.☺

Strawberry-Banana Cream

1 cup frozen sliced bananas
1 cup frozen strawberries
½ teaspoon pure vanilla extract
¼ to ½ cup milk (dairy or non-dairy)

In a food processor, pulse fruit until coarsely chopped. Add milk a little at a time through top of processor, and puree until creamy. Serve immediately, or freeze in individual-size containers for later.

Yield: 4 servings

Amasake Cream

1 cup frozen peach slices
1 cup frozen raspberries
¼ to ½ cup amasake

In a food processor, pulse fruit until coarsely chopped. Add amasake a little at a time through top of processor, and puree until creamy. Serve immediately, or freeze in individual-size containers for later.

Yield: 4 servings

Avocado Cream

I tried avocado ice cream at a local avocado festival, and it was yummy. My version is made without dairy or sugar. This unlikely combination is incredibly rich, creamy, and delicious.

1 cup frozen banana slices
1 medium ripe avocado, diced (about ⅔ cup)

Chop bananas into small pieces in a food processor. Add avocado. Puree until creamy. Serve immediately, or freeze in individual-size containers for later.

Yield: 3 to 4 servings

Freezing Fruit

Frozen fruit is essential for Better Than Ice Cream and makes colder, thicker smoothies. Start at least six hours before you are planning to use the fruit.

Apricot, Nectarine, Peach: Remove pit and slice
Banana: Peel and slice
Berries: Hull and leave whole
Mango: Remove peel and pit, cut into chunks
Melon, Papaya: Remove peel and pulp, cut into chunks

Lay prepared fruit on baking sheet and place in freezer until completely frozen. Remove fruit from pan. Store in freezer bags or containers.

☺Tip: Freezing is a great way to use up ripe fruit that might otherwise go bad. Frozen fruit keeps for months. Buy extra fruit in season to freeze so you'll always be ready to make smoothies or ices.☺

Baby Pops

Homemade popsicles are a healthful treat for your child. Unlike juice, which can be gulped down creating a sugar rush, popsicles must be licked or sucked slowly. This gives the body time to adjust to the sugar intake. Use pure, unsweetened juice alone or pureed with fruit or yogurt.

Preparing Popsicles

Pour popsicle mixture into ice cube trays. Place a plastic straw section, dixie spoon, or wooden popsicle stick in each cube, and freeze until solid. These are the perfect size for young children. As they get older, you may want to use plastic popsicle trays.

☺Tip: All of the Smoothie (page 119) and Better Than Ice Cream (page 110) recipes can be frozen as popsicles.☺

Juice Pops

Pour **1 cup pure, unsweetened juice** into ice cube tray. Freeze until solid.

Yield: 14

Yogurt Pops

Pour **½ cup plain yogurt** and **½ cup juice** into jar, and shake until blended. Pour into ice cube tray. Freeze until solid.

Yield: 14

Cakes, Bars, and Cookies

Zucchini Cake

¾ cup raisins
Boiling water
2¼ cups whole wheat, brown rice, or barley flour
1 tablespoon baking powder
½ teaspoon sea salt
½ teaspoon ground cinnamon
¼ teaspoon ground nutmeg
½ cup raw or toasted wheat germ
½ cup chopped walnuts
3 tablespoons honey, brown rice syrup, or pure
   maple syrup
3 tablespoons oil
1 egg, beaten
1 teaspoon grated lemon peel
2 tablespoons lemon juice (optional)
1½ to 2 cups grated zucchini

Preheat oven to 375°. Oil an 8-inch or 9-inch square baking pan. Place raisins in a glass measuring cup. Fill with hot water to the 1-cup level. Set aside. Sift together flour, baking powder, salt, cinnamon, and nutmeg. Stir in wheat germ and walnuts. In a separate bowl, beat together honey, oil, egg, lemon peel, and juice. Mix in zucchini, raisins, and raisin water. Stir the dry ingredients into the egg mixture. Pour into prepared pan. Bake 40 to 50 minutes, or until a knife inserted in center comes out clean. Frost cooled cake with Cream Cheese Frosting (recipe follows) or Pineapple-Yogurt Frosting (page 69).

Yield: 16 servings

Cream Cheese Frosting

In food processor or mixer, beat **8 ounces cream cheese**, **½ teaspoon pure vanilla extract**, and enough **apple juice concentrate or juice** to create a frosting consistency with a slightly sweet taste. Maple syrup or honey also work well.

Yield: 1 cup

Almond Butter Raisin Chews

Your children will love to shape these sugar-free treats, especially if you try one of the variations.

½ cup raisins
½ cup almond or peanut butter
⅓ cup dry milk powder (soy is fine)
1 teaspoon vanilla extract
1 tablespoon water

Grind raisins in food processor with metal blade. Add remaining ingredients, and process until smooth. Shape into 16 balls, and chill.

Yield: 16

Note: If you don't have a food processor, chop raisins by hand, and mix all ingredients in a bowl with your hands.

Variation: Roll balls in coconut flakes, sesame seeds, or chopped nuts before refrigerating.

Fig Bars

These are so much better than any store-bought fig bar.

Filling:
   1 cup tightly packed figs
   Boiling water
   ¼ cup orange or apple juice

Dough:
   ½ cup butter or non-hydrogenated margarine,
      softened
   ½ cup honey or brown rice syrup
   1 egg
   ½ teaspoon grated lemon rind
   1 tablespoon lemon juice
   3 cups whole wheat flour
   1 teaspoon baking powder
   ½ teaspoon baking soda

To prepare filling, place figs in a small heat-proof bowl. Pour just enough boiling water over figs to cover them. Let figs sit 30 minutes. Drain water, and grind figs in food processor. While processor is running, add juice through top and puree until smooth.

Preheat oven to 400°. Oil a 9 x 13-inch baking pan. To prepare dough, cream butter or margarine and sweetener together until light and fluffy. Beat in eggs, lemon rind, and juice. Add flour, baking powder, and baking soda. Mix well.

Divide dough in half. Roll out one half, and press it into the bottom of prepared baking pan. Spread filling evenly over dough. Roll out remaining dough and lay it over top of filling. Press it down firmly. Bake 12 to 15 minutes, or until golden brown around edges and dough springs back when touched lightly.

Yield: 48

☺Tip: Fig-soaking water is great in smoothies.☺

Carrot Cake Sprout Cookies

As wheat berries germinate, the starch turns into grain sugar (maltose). With a little fruit to enhance the sweetness, you can make delicious cookies without sugar, flour, butter, or eggs. Most natural food stores carry untreated seeds for sprouting.

> **1 cup soft wheat berries, sprouted for two days
> (instructions follow)**
> **1 carrot, sliced**
> **4 dates (pits removed)**
> **¼ cup raisins**
> **1 banana, peeled and sliced**
> **1 tablespoon tahini, almond butter, or peanut butter**
> **1 tablespoon unsweetened coconut flakes**
> **1 teaspoon ground cinnamon**
> **¼ teaspoon ground nutmeg**

Preheat oven to 250°. In food processor, grind sprouts and carrots until they start to form a paste. Add remaining ingredients and process until smooth. With wet hands, shape the dough into tablespoon-size balls. Roll balls in sesame seeds and flatten slightly on unoiled cookie sheet. Cookies can be packed close together because they do not spread. Bake 1½ to 2 hours. They are done when firm but still moist.

Yield: About 2 dozen

Sprouting Wheat Berries

Pour **1 cup soft wheat berries** into a quart-size jar. Add **2 cups water.** Place a piece of cheesecloth over top of jar and secure with a rubber band. Let seeds soak in a warm, dark place for 12 hours.

Pour off water. Rinse soaked seeds by filling the jar with water and inverting it to drain through cheesecloth. Position the jar at a 45-degree angle, mouth side down, to allow excess moisture to drain. Place jar out of direct sunlight. Rinse sprouts at least twice daily to provide them with water and wash away by-products of growth.

After two days, or when the sprouts are about as long as the wheat berries, remove cheesecloth and pour the sprouts into a colander. Rinse the sprouts and let drain for a few hours until sprouts are moist but not wet. Wet sprouts will make the dough too loose, and dry sprouts will not form a dough.

Cream Cheese Bon Bons

These are absolutely delectable and so easy to make.

¾ cup walnuts
½ cup raisins
8 ounces cream cheese
1 teaspoon vanilla

Mince walnuts in food processor with metal blade. Pour walnuts into a shallow dish. Place raisins in food processor and pulse until they are coarsely chopped. Add cream cheese and vanilla. Process until smooth. Form cream cheese mixture into 1-inch balls, and roll in minced walnuts. Keep balls refrigerated.

Yield: About 1½ dozen

Beverages

Sesame Seed Milk

Sesame seeds are an extremely absorbable source of calcium. Substitute seed milk for dairy or soy milk in any recipe.

½ **cup raw sesame seeds (hulled or unhulled)**
2 **cups water, or 1¼ cups water and ¾ cups apple juice**

Grind sesame seeds dry to powder in blender. Add liquid and blend until smooth.

Use *as is* in smoothies, cereals, or cooking. For a smooth drinking texture, pour through a fine strainer or cheesecloth. The pulp can be added to hot or cold cereal, or used as a facial scrub (for you, not baby).

Yield: 2 cups

Sunflower Seed Milk

Sunflower seeds are a good source of vitamins D and E. Substitute seed milk for dairy or soy milk in any recipe.

½ **cup raw sunflower seeds (hulled)**
2 **cups water**
2 **teaspoons pure maple syrup, molasses or honey (optional)**

Grind seeds dry to powder in blender. Add water and optional sweetener and blend until smooth.

Use *as is* in smoothies, cereals, or cooking. For a smooth drinking texture, pour through a fine strainer or cheesecloth. The pulp can be added to hot or cold cereal, or used as a facial scrub (for you, not baby).

Yield: 2 cups

Smoothies

Smoothies are a good alternative to juice. They are still sweet, but since whole fruit is used your child gets the fiber too. Try adding vegetables to smoothies. No one will know! Add yogurt, tofu, nut butter, or nutritional yeast flakes for extra protein and calcium. Smoothies make great snacks or a quick summer breakfast. Try freezing them as popsicles too.

☺Tip: Smoothies are thicker than juice and may clog a sippy cup. Try a covered straw-cup instead.☺

Sesame-Banana Shake

¼ cup raw sesame seeds (hulled or unhulled)
1 banana, cut into chunks (fresh or frozen)
1 cup water
Pinch ground nutmeg (optional)

Grind seeds dry to powder in blender. Add remaining ingredients and puree until smooth.

Yield: 1 to 2 servings

Vitamin C Supreme

2 cups watermelon chunks or 1 cup orange juice
6 strawberries (fresh or frozen)
¼ cup parsley, kale, broccoli, or cabbage

Put all ingredients in blender and puree until smooth.

Yield: 2 to 3 servings

Creamy Greens

This beautiful, green smoothie is so delicious. It's a super way to get your kids to eat kale.

½ cup pineapple or pineapple-coconut juice
½ cup milk (dairy or non-dairy)
1 banana, frozen
1 handful kale
1 tablespoon nutritional yeast flakes

Place ingredients in blender and puree until smooth.

Yield: 2 to 3 servings

☺Tip: Frozen fruit makes thicker, colder smoothies. See instructions for freezing your own fruit on page 111.☺

Beta Carotene Special

This smoothie supplies vitamin A, which is important for good eyesight and night vision.

2 cups cantaloupe melon chunks or 1 cup juice
1 peach or nectarine, fresh or frozen
1 to 2 apricots, fresh or frozen
½ raw sweet potato or 1 carrot, sliced

Place all ingredients in blender and puree until smooth.

Yield: 2 to 3 servings

Sources and Resources

Books

Infant Care

Your Baby and Child from Birth to Age Five, New Edition, Revised and Expanded, by Penelope Leach. New York: Alfred A. Knopf, 1997.

What to Expect In The First Year, by Arlene Eisenberg, Heidi E. Murkoff, and Sandee Eisenberg Hathaway. New York: Workman Publishing Company, 1996.

Infant Health

The Holistic Pediatrician: A Parents' Comprehensive Guide to Safe and Effective Therapies for the Twenty-Five Most Common Childhood Ailments, by Kathi J. Kemper, MD. San Francisco, CA: HarperCollins, 1996.

Smart Medicine for a Healthier Child: A Practical A-to-Z Reference to Natural and Conventional Treatments for Infants and Children, by Janet Zand, LAc, OMD; Rachel Walton, RN; and Bob Rountree, MD. Garden City Park, NY: Avery Publishing Group, 1994.

Infant Nutrition

The Crazy Makers: How the Food Industry Is Destroying Our Brains and Harming Our Children, by Carol Simontacchi. New York: Tarcher/Putnam, 2000.

New Vegetarian Baby, by Sharon K. Yntema and Christine H. Beard. Ithaca, NY: McBooks Press, 2000.

Natural Foods

The New Whole Foods Encyclopedia: A Comprehensive Resource for Healthy Eating, by Rebecca Wood. New York: Penguin, 1999.

The New Laurel's Kitchen, by Laurel Robertson, Carol Flinders, and Brian Ruppenthal. Berkeley, CA: Ten Speed Press, 1986.

Rodale's Basic Natural Foods Cookbook, edited by Charles Gerras. New York: Simon & Schuster, 1984.

Sproutman's Kitchen Garden Cookbook, by Steve Meyerowitz. Great Barrington, MA: Sproutman Publications, 1999.

Organizations

Infant Health and Nutrition

American Academy of Pediatrics
141 Northwest Point Blvd.
Elk Grove Village, IL 60007-1098
847-969-2267
www.aap.org

American Association of Naturopathic Physicians
8201 Greensboro Drive, Suite 300
McLean, VA 22102
877-969-2267
www.naturopathic.org

Society of Certified Nutritionists
2111 Bridgeport Way W, #2
University Place, WA 98466
800-342-8037
www.certifiednutritionist.com

Organic Food

Environmental Working Group
1718 Connecticut Ave. NW, Suite 600
Washington, DC 20009
202-667-6982
www.ewg.org

True Food Network
702 H Street NW, Suite 300
Washington, DC 20001
www.truefoodnow.org

Index

About the Author

Cathe Olson has studied nutrition and cooking both formally and informally for fifteen years. She is a vegetarian, macrobiotic, and whole foods chef. Cathe has cooked at natural food restaurants and delis in both the San Francisco Bay and Central Coast areas of California. She is the author of the booklet *Beyond Rice Cereal: Healthy Food Your Infant and Toddler Will Love to Eat*, as well as numerous articles on nutrition and healthy eating.

Cathe, her husband Gary, and daughters Aimie and Emily raise organic vegetables, herbs, fruit, and free-range chickens on their farm in Suey Creek, California.

Cathe welcomes your questions and comments. Email her at cathe@simplynaturalbooks.com or contact her through the website:

http://www.simplynaturalbooks.com